STAY SANE

IN AN INSANE WORLD

GREG HARDEN

WITH **STEVE HAMILTON**

STAY SANE
IN AN INSANE WORLD

HOW TO CONTROL THE CONTROLLABLES AND THRIVE

FOREWORD BY

TOM BRADY

SEVEN-TIME SUPER BOWL CHAMPION

BLACK STONE PUBLISHING

Printed in the United States of America

First edition: 2023
ISBN 978-1-6650-9241-8
Self-Help / Self-Management / General

Version 1

Blackstone Publishing
31 Mistletoe Rd.
Ashland, OR 97520

www.BlackstonePublishing.com

TABLE OF CONTENTS

AUTHOR'S NOTE vii

FOREWORD TOM BRADY ix

CHAPTER 1: DARE TO BE DIFFERENT 1

CHAPTER 2: WHAT MAKES *THEM* DIFFERENT? 6

CHAPTER 3: CONTROL THE CONTROLLABLES! 13

CHAPTER 4: WHO WILL ANSWER? 19

CHAPTER 5: DREAM BIG, BELIEVE BIG, BECOME BIG 23

TESTIMONIAL: DESMOND HOWARD 28

CHAPTER 6: WHAT DOES SUCCESS LOOK LIKE? 31

CHAPTER 7: THE DEMON ON YOUR LEFT SHOULDER:

   SELF-*DEFEATING* ATTITUDES AND BEHAVIORS 38

CHAPTER 8: THE ANGEL ON YOUR RIGHT SHOULDER:

   SELF-*SUPPORTING* ATTITUDES AND BEHAVIORS 47

CHAPTER 9: CREATING YOUR IDEAL SELF 58

TESTIMONIAL: MICHELLE MCMAHON 63

CHAPTER 10: ONLY AN ASSERTIVE YOU CAN BE A SUCCESSFUL YOU 66

TESTIMONIAL: EMILY LINE 71

CHAPTER 11: THE 100 PERCENT CHALLENGE 75

CHAPTER 12: ADAPT OR DIE! 80

CHAPTER 13: YOUR SPORT IS WHAT YOU DO, NOT WHO YOU ARE 85

TESTIMONIAL: MICHAEL PARKE 91

CHAPTER 14: WHAT DO YOU DO WHEN YOU LOSE EVERYTHING? 93

TESTIMONIAL: WARDE MANUEL 96

CHAPTER 15: A MATTER OF TRUST 98

CHAPTER 16: THE TWO KINDS OF LOVE 102

CHAPTER 17: GET OUT OF YOUR OWN WAY! 106

TESTIMONIAL: COOPER MARODY 112

CHAPTER 18: SWOT YOURSELF 115

CHAPTER 19: COMMIT, IMPROVE, MAINTAIN 120

TESTIMONIAL: JONATHAN SATOVSKY 124

CHAPTER 20: HOW TO CREATE BAD HABITS . . . AND GOOD ONES 127

CHAPTER 21: IT'S PERFECTLY OKAY NOT TO BE PERFECT 130

CHAPTER 22: THE VALUE OF A SHORT MEMORY 134

CHAPTER 23: A PERMANENT SOLUTION TO A TEMPORARY PROBLEM 137

CHAPTER 24: FAITH-BASED AND SOLUTION-FOCUSED 140

CHAPTER 25: FEAR, COURAGE, AND "BUCK FEVER" 142

CHAPTER 26: EXPOSE YOUR VAMPIRES TO THE LIGHT 147

TESTIMONIAL: ANN WELCH BRAUN 150

CHAPTER 27: . . . BY ITS COVER 153

CHAPTER 28: THE TEAM, THE TEAM, THE TEAM 157

TESTIMONIAL: ERIK CAMPBELL 161

CHAPTER 29: ONE MORE TEAM . . . AND THE ULTIMATE CHALLENGE 163

TESTIMONIAL: WALEED SAMAHA 167

CHAPTER 30: SAY THANK YOU (AND THEN SHUT YOUR MOUTH) 170

CHAPTER 31: WHISPERS AND BRICKS 174

CHAPTER 32: FACING THE CHALLENGE OF PUBLIC SPEAKING 176

CHAPTER 33: WHEN YOU'RE INTERVIEWING SOMEONE,

   LET THEM TELL YOU WHO THEY ARE 178

CHAPTER 34: WHEN YOU'RE BEING INTERVIEWED, TURN IT AROUND! 181

CHAPTER 35: IF YOU HAPPEN TO BE A GOLFER 183

CHAPTER 36: PLEASE REMEMBER THESE SEVEN THINGS 188

TESTIMONIAL: STEVE HAMILTON 190

CHAPTER 37: THE CHALLENGE: 192

DEDICATION AND ACKNOWLEDGMENTS 195

ABOUT THE AUTHORS 197

AUTHOR'S NOTE

This is *not* a conventional "how-to" book with a systematic, step-by-step formula detailing what you must do to be rich and successful.

This book will require you to *think* and to find for yourself the specific stories and pieces of advice that you can relate to. *You* must identify the chapters that genuinely teach your mind and your heart. I'm asking you to explore and to find a story, a phrase—*anything* that you can latch on to—and then let it help you become the person you've always dreamed of becoming.

One of the most important things that I emphasize and teach is that if your life is going to work, it will be because of your decision-making, your ability to have healthy relationships, and your ability to recognize and take total control over those things you can control.

It has been uniquely exciting to work with a lot of seventeen- to twenty-three-year-olds throughout my career and to challenge each of them to let the adolescent child start taking a back seat to the young adult. Trying to convince them that if you want to be the best, you have to develop yourself in more than just one area. Imagine the challenge. I have this student in my office and I'm trying to explain that the best way to become a better *athlete* is to become a better *person*.

Of course, it's the same truth for anyone, at any age, in any walk of life. You can't become the best sales rep, the best manager, the best parent, the best spouse, the best *anything*, until you become the best *person* you can possibly be.

It's a tough sell sometimes, but I've learned that I have to push people to understand that we all come with certain baggage. We all have our own stories in our lives, of where we came from, hardships or trauma we've endured, people we've known, loved, or lost. I've known so many winners, champions, All-American this or that, who turn out to be real human beings with stories that would make you weep. They struggle with the same things that you and I struggle with every day.

Whether you are seventeen or seventy, there is a child or adolescent in you who needs your love and your acceptance. At the same time, there's an *adult* inside you who needs to understand which attitudes and behaviors are working and which ones are sabotaging your dreams.

In the end, the real mission of this book—my objective, my *obsession*—is to help you become the world's greatest expert on one subject: yourself.

Greg Harden

TOM BRADY

FOREWORD

Seven-time Super Bowl Champion • Five-time Super Bowl MVP • Three-time league MVP • Fourteen-time Pro-Bowler • Sixth-round pick in the 2000 NFL draft • 199th selection overall (behind six other quarterbacks)

"What I learned from Greg is still a part of who I am today."

Some people think that going away to college makes you an adult. But when I came to the University of Michigan in 1995, I was still a sheltered kid from San Mateo, California, the youngest in a family of four children, and the only boy. It was my first time in the Midwest. I had very little life experience and not much perspective. I needed to grow up fast, but I didn't know how.

I arrived on campus wanting to play football. But things didn't go according to my plan. There were six guys ahead of me on the depth chart. I believed I wasn't being given the same opportunities to succeed as some other players were. I thought I'd never get to play football here. In my mind, it was very possible I'd chosen the wrong school. I was frustrated and disheartened. But as the saying goes, when the student is ready, the teacher appears.

Greg Harden had been at the University of Michigan since 1986, working mostly with the football and basketball teams. His job title was Director of Athletic Counseling, but you would never have known it. He was just another guy on the sidelines during practices, and in meal rooms and on team road trips. At one point during the season, Greg told me he'd been watching me. Maybe the two of us could find some time to spend together? Hey, what about 8:00 a.m. next Tuesday? I didn't know I'd just met a great, lifelong mentor, and one of the greatest treasures and resources for student athletes that the University of Michigan will ever know.

Whenever I think of Greg, I picture his infectious smile, his charisma, his wisdom, his off-the-charts IQ and EQ, the natural ability he has to connect with a huge variety of people. Greg was—and is—a progressive thinker. He's always been ahead of his time. He took in the whole picture, meaning that along with the physical and mental parts of being a student athlete, Greg also saw me as an emotional being. What I *really* needed to do was to direct my emotions to the right place.

Greg was extremely caring, but he wasn't a coddler. Over the next few months and years, he pushed me to wake up and grow up. With Greg's help, I transformed from a player who always believed that circumstances were stacked against him, into one who competed with energy, enthusiasm, a positive outlook, and an unshakable belief in himself. Greg never allowed me (or anybody) to play the victim. *If it was to be, it was up to me.* By giving me the tools I needed to succeed on my own terms, so I could become the best player and person I could be, he rewired my outlook and maybe even my psyche.

More than twenty years later, I still think back on Greg's teachings. *Quit focusing on all the things you can't control. Focus on being the best version of yourself. Work as hard as you can. If you're only going to get one rep, do it perfectly. I don't give a shit about what's "fair!" Go out there, embrace your teammates, be a leader, and do the best you can!*

As time went on, I started looking at football through a new lens. *If it was to be, it was up to me.* Greg reminded me it's not supposed to be easy. The obstacle in your path isn't there to create frustration or make you doubt yourself, or storm off, or quit. The obstacle is the way. Difficulty is an *advantage.* The more obstacles in your path, the higher the odds you'll succeed. Why? Because in the face of those obstacles, a lot of other guys will just back down. That mindset is a big reason why, early in my football career when I was drafted by the New England Patriots, rather than tell myself I'd never get the opportunity to play, I thought, *Okay, let's go, it's time to see what I'm really made of. If I'm going to be the best, I have to beat the best.*

What I learned from Greg is still a part of who I am today. If my team is down 10 points with a minute and a half left to play, that's an opportunity. There's nothing wrong with losing late in a game. What's there to worry about? There's nothing to lose—*so why not just go for it?* Is there a better opportunity for your team to come back and win the game? A better moment to dig deep, focus, and show your mental toughness? A better opportunity for you to learn about who you really are? *That's* where greatness lies. *That's* the glory of sport. *That's* how Greg sees life.

It goes beyond the field, too. If you're in a place in life you don't want to be, it's up to you to make it better. To reframe it by focusing on the positive, and approaching it with enthusiasm. In the end, your positivity and enthusiasm will contribute to creating the outcome you're after. Once you apply this mindset to all aspects of your life, you corner fear. Fear basically has nowhere to go.

For his whole career, Greg has practiced what he's preached. He's kept growing, learning, getting better, getting things done, putting in the work and living up to his own high standards. If NFL and college teams embraced Greg's wisdom, a lot of lives would be positively impacted and transformed. The world needs more Greg Hardens. Meanwhile, I'm one of the many hundreds of student athletes who were lucky enough to work alongside the original.

Tom Brady

CHAPTER 1

DARE TO BE DIFFERENT

If you read the outside of this book, you know that I've been counseling athletes at the University of Michigan for over thirty years. Along the way, I've had the privilege of helping a few special athletes you've heard of—think Tom Brady, Michael Phelps, Desmond Howard—and a lot more athletes who have done things just as great or greater, though with maybe a little less widespread public fanfare.

To put myself in this position helping student athletes, coaches, counselors, entrepreneurs, Fortune 100 companies—as well as addicts and criminals—to become the world's greatest experts on themselves so that they could become the best versions of themselves, I had to start by doing this for myself.

When I was a very young man of fourteen years, I had this uncle who would come by the house just to harass me. When I was eight, I thought he was amusing and delightful. By fourteen, I couldn't stand him.

He came by one day, and he was picking on me, as usual, poking and prodding and doing everything he could to get on my last nerve. And it was working. Then he finally said to me, "What do you want to be when you grow up?"

I thought about it for a few seconds, and then I answered: "I want to be different."

"No, seriously, boy," he said. "What are you gonna do when you're an adult?"

"Seriously," I said. "I want to be *different*."

Which was my indirect, almost polite way of saying, "I don't want to be like you."

Think back to when you were fourteen. Looking back on all the adults who were in your life then, did you really want to grow up to be just like them? From my own fourteen-year-old vantage point, so many of the adults I had seen were constantly complaining and whining and moaning and groaning. Why would I want to sign up for that?

They were too often *miserable, negative*, and *depressed*, and not only that, they were recruiting me to be exactly the same way. "This is the way the world works, kid. You gotta pick a side. Pick a color, pick a religion, pick a political party. You gotta figure out how to make money and consume everything, and most importantly, you gotta remember to always think only about yourself."

At fourteen years old, I *knew* I wanted something different. If only I'd been smart enough to hold on to that simple idea . . .

But instead of having the strength and wisdom to become my own best version of myself, I let the times I was living in mold my character. It was a tumultuous time in this country, and "the hate that hate made" tried to consume me every day. I wasn't just negative, miserable, and depressed. I was angry at the whole world. I was truly and profoundly my own worst enemy, and the only thing that exceeded my ignorance was my arrogance.

I was programmed—and socialized—to be prejudiced, to be sexist, to be a homophobe and a xenophobe, to hate entire *groups* of people. I was recruited out of my high school in Detroit to run track at the University of Michigan, and I arrived on campus *committed* to being angry, *committed* to being filled with hate. What I wasn't committed to was running track or making smart choices in my life. Two years later, I was out of school, with a child on the way, working at a steel mill—cleaning out the coils underneath a furnace, wearing a rubber suit in 105 degrees.

I had to take a hard look at my life then. Ask myself if I was really doing what I wanted to do with my time here on earth. It was a long, long journey to finally get back to that mindset I had at fourteen. To this dream I had of being *different*.

I decided to give school another try. I was twenty-eight, older than most of my peers, when I finally graduated with a master's degree in social work. I started to build a career by counseling people who were struggling with addiction to alcohol and drugs. I never dreamed I'd ever be a part of the world of athletics again—until the day I told Bo Schembechler I didn't want to talk to his football players. Instead of dismissing me as a fool, he asked to *meet* me! (See "Chapter 15: A Matter of Trust.")

In the three decades since, I've had the privilege of working with thousands of individuals who allowed me to dare them to believe in themselves. And no matter who they were or where they came from, I told them all the same thing I told Tom Brady the first time he sat in my office: *If you don't believe in yourself, why should I believe in you?*

You'll hear me use that phrase a few more times throughout this book. You'll also hear me ask you to *Practice, Train, and Rehearse.* Because if you practice, train, and rehearse believing in yourself, it will become second nature. If you practice, train, and rehearse giving 100 percent, 100 percent of the time, that will become second nature, too.

But if you practice, train, and rehearse being negative, miserable, and depressed, well, that's what you'll be good at.

You'll also hear me talk about how important it is for you to learn to *control the controllables.* Because there are so many things in life you can't control—things that other people do, or ways that they try to make you feel—and just a few important things that you *can* control, most importantly your own actions, reactions, and feelings.

This message is more important today than ever as we watch this country, and the entire world, struggle with not one but two historic crises at the same time.

Our ability to keep functioning, both together and as individuals, as *everything* gets turned upside down all around us—to focus on those things that we *can* control when everything else seems to be spinning completely out of control—is more valuable right now than it has ever been. I'll have a lot more to say about this in "Chapter 3: Control the Controllables!"

In the end, all I'm trying to do is build you up, encourage you to stay positive in a negative world, and help you *stay sane in an insane world*.

I want you to become the best friend you ever had in your life, because your very best friend *has* to be you.

I want you to become the world's greatest expert on yourself, so you'll have the knowledge and the power to become the very best *version* of yourself.

Or as my amazing wife, Shelia Harden, likes to say, "I want you to live your best life *now*."

And when you're done with this book, I've got something very important to ask you in the very last chapter.

So let's get started.

I CAN'T TEACH **TOM BRADY**
HOW TO **THROW THE BALL.**
I CAN'T TEACH **DESMOND HOWARD**
HOW TO **CATCH THE BALL.**
I CAN'T TEACH **MICHAEL PHELPS**
HOW TO DO **A PERFECT FLIP TURN.**
ALL I CAN DO **IS TEACH YOU**
HOW TO BECOME
THE WORLD'S GREATEST
EXPERT ON ONE SUBJECT:
YOURSELF.

—GREG HARDEN

CHAPTER 2

WHAT MAKES *THEM* DIFFERENT?

It was December 1999. The annual "Michigan Football Bust," where the past season is reviewed and the seniors are recognized and given their M rings. It's a big event, with all the players' families, the coaches, and many of the team's fans.

When the event was over, two parents approached me: Tom Brady, Sr. and his wife, Galynn. Mr. Brady shook my hand and said, "We just wanted to say thank you so much for what you did for our son. You really helped change his life, and we are eternally grateful."

"Look, let me tell you something," I said to them. "I appreciate everything you're saying, but I only did for your son what he *allowed* me to do. Because of how you raised him, he was open to growing mentally, physically, and spiritually. To being guided. His respect for authority, his understanding of how to listen and take direction—that all comes from you. So I want to thank *you* for what you did to prepare him to be one of the most coachable kids I've ever had at Michigan."

I wasn't just saying it to be nice. I meant every word. I'll talk more about Tom Brady in "Chapter 4: Who Will Answer?" and about how I challenged him to tell me how he expected coaches to believe in him if he didn't believe in himself. At that banquet, the regular season was over, but Brady was still preparing to lead the team into the Orange Bowl, where he would overcome three 14-point deficits to beat Alabama 35-34 in overtime—still one of the best performances I've ever seen by a college quarterback.

If Tom Brady was one of the most coachable kids I had ever met, it was Desmond Howard who set the standard. I talk about him in "Chapter 5: Dream Big, Believe Big, Become Big." He was a few years before Brady, and at the time I had never met anyone quite like him. Of all the athletes I have worked with, in all the sports at Michigan, Desmond Howard was the one kid who would look me right in the eye and say, "Tell me what to do. Tell me every mistake you've ever made, so I can avoid them."

"I'm not like the other guys on the team," he told me on another occasion. "If you tell me, 'Don't touch that because it will burn you,' I guarantee you I won't touch that thing! Unlike a lot of my friends, my teammates, if you tell me something won't work, I'll believe you. *Just tell me what works.*"

This all came after we got him through a tough period in his life, when he was a sophomore, playing a new position, and actually wondering if he should transfer to another school. When I told him that this "geographical cure" was just a fantasy and that he needed to stay at Michigan and work on becoming the best athlete on the team, he *listened* to me. And he stayed.

And he went on to become the first Heisman Trophy winner at Michigan in fifty-one years.

What I didn't know when I first met Desmond was that he had been studying me ever since I first talked to the football team when he was a freshman. A year and a half later, he finally came to talk to me, and I've been talking to him ever since, through eleven years as a professional football player—and the only special-teams player ever to be named Super Bowl MVP—and even now as a fixture on ESPN's *College GameDay*.

The first thing that Tom Brady and Desmond Howard had in common—the one thing shared by some of the biggest stars and highest-level performers I've worked with over the years—is that they were *hungry* for input, *hungry* for information, *hungry* to learn.

They were *coachable* in every sense of the word.

Now, when we get to Michael Phelps in "Chapter 6: What Does

Success Look Like?,'" I'll be talking about a unique time in the young man's life, when he had already become an Olympic medalist after giving up his whole life to the sport of swimming. He may have been rebelling at age nineteen, having never had a real childhood, but from age four to eighteen, he was coachable as hell. Just ask the US swim coach, Bob Bowman. Even though God gifted him with the perfect swimmer's body, Michael Phelps would never have become the most decorated Olympian in history if he weren't an absolute *sponge* (water, swimming, sponge— sorry) for every tiny detail on how to maximize his talent in the water.

So beyond *coachability*, the second thing these high performers have in common is what I'm going to call *a belief in the process of self-improvement*. I talk more about this topic in "Chapter 19: Commit, Improve, Maintain." It's a three-step process in which you *commit* to doing what it takes to make yourself better, then you do the hard work to *improve* your performance in EVERYTHING you do, and then you *maintain* that performance over time.

A simple idea, right? But how many people really do this?

I mean, *really* do this?

In Tom Brady's 2017 book, *The TB12 Method: How to Achieve a Lifetime of Sustained Peak Performance*, he shares the story of his "secret" Friday-morning workout, when he'd carve out some personal one-on-one time with the Patriots' strength-and-conditioning coach:

> With every level you reach, everyone gets faster, stronger, and better, and I had to work really hard just to be competitive. That's why every Friday at 6:00 a.m., when no one else was around, I worked with [him] doing speed and footwork drills, trying to close the gap between me and my teammates.

Now, getting up early on one Friday morning didn't suddenly allow Tom Brady to "close the gap." But if you do something today that improves your performance by one-tenth of 1 percent . . .

And then you do it again tomorrow.

And then again the next day.

We're talking compound interest—just think where you'll be a year from now!

So: coachability, a desire to learn. Believing in, and committing yourself to, the process of self-improvement. That's two things. Here's the third, and maybe the most important of all. And yet, maybe the hardest thing to define . . .

Sometimes I call it an *edge*. Sometimes I call it an *extra gear*. Maybe you have your own word for it, but I think you know what I'm talking about here.

On football Saturdays, I usually sit down close to the field, right behind the Michigan bench. I interact with some of the players during the game, doing everything I can to give encouragement. But sometimes, a special player will come along who turns everything around and gives *me* the encouragement.

Such a player was Charles Woodson, another Heisman Trophy winner who would go on to become arguably the best defensive back in the history of the game, at both the college *and* professional level. (In fact, he was just inducted into the NFL Hall of Fame on the first ballot as I was finishing this book!)

We were home against Iowa, the sixth game of the season after starting the season 5-0, including big wins over Colorado and Notre Dame. But this game was not going our way, and Iowa was ahead 21-7 at halftime. As the players came out to start the second half, Charles Woodson caught my eye, walked over closer to me, and said, "Don't worry, G, we got this."

Now, understand, this wasn't a basketball game. It wasn't as if Woodson could put the whole team on his back, go out, and score 40 points in the second half. In fact, he wasn't even an offensive player! He played defense! How does a defensive player say, "We got this," when his team is 14 points down?

He hit a switch in his mind and his body to elevate his performance to another level. And just as importantly, he directly inspired his teammates to do the same.

Final score: Michigan 28, Iowa 24.

The team would finish that season undefeated, with Woodson returning a punt for a touchdown in the Ohio State game. When they went on to beat Washington State in the Rose Bowl, it was Michigan's first national football championship since 1948.

What I'm trying to tell you here is that sometimes you see somebody performing at the highest level you can imagine. *And then they kick it up into another gear.*

Because they *have to.*

Because the circumstances require it.

Because it's the only way they're going to win.

It happens, not within the context of only one game, but over an entire *season*, over an entire *career.* When Tom Brady had to share his starting job at Michigan in his senior year . . .

It made him better.

When he fell to the sixth round of the NFL draft, finally being picked number 199 . . .

It made him better.

Even now, at forty-three years old, a seven-time Super Bowl champion, he still plays like he's trying to prove something. (This was another story that was changing even as I was finishing this book. Tom was preparing to appear in his tenth Super Bowl, the first with his new team . . . And you know how that turned out.) He's still giving 100 percent, 100 percent of the time. ("Chapter 11: The 100 Percent Challenge.")

That's the edge, the extra gear I'm talking about. The ability to turn it up when you need to, even when it feels as if you were *already* giving 100 percent. To *decide* that you're going to win. To *decide* that you're going to find a way to push yourself, and everyone else around you, to another level.

To *decide* that you're going to take all the failures and setbacks in your life and turn them into *fuel.*

Like Michael Jordan, coming back to the NBA after the murder of his father and after struggling to become a pro baseball player, and leading the Bulls to three more consecutive championships.

Or Tiger Woods, convalescing from his *fourth* back surgery and wondering if he would ever be able to swing a club again or even walk right, working his way back to the top of the game and winning the Masters at age forty-three.

Or Mario Lemieux, missing two months of the NHL season with Hodgkin's lymphoma, nearly dying from it, then coming back to win the scoring title.

And let's be clear, it's not just men who own these stories:

Figure skater Nancy Kerrigan, attacked by a man with a club, coming back to medal in the 1994 Winter Olympics.

Gymnast Kerri Strug, vaulting on a severely injured ankle to help the United States secure the team gold medal at the 1996 Olympics.

Tennis player Monica Seles, stabbed on the court by a deranged fan of her rival, then coming back to medal in the 2000 Olympics.

We love these comeback stories. They *inspire* us. But I want you to be more than inspired. I want you to realize that this ability to dig down and find that extra gear when you really need it is something that *you already have inside yourself.*

I know it. You know it. Take a moment right now. Think back on such a moment in your life, when you had to *decide* not to quit. When you had to *decide* to give even more than what you thought was your best.

Now imagine making that determination, that *extra gear,* a permanent part of you. Something you can call upon whenever you need it. Something that will propel you to victory—or, at the very least, force your opponent to find his or her extra gear just to have a chance at beating you.

That's what makes a champion.

I've tried to cover three important topics here, but please also remember what I *didn't* say. In this whole discussion of "What makes them different?" did I ever mention anything about 2 percent body fat, or a forty-inch vertical leap, or a 4.3-second forty-yard dash? I did not, and in fact, I can point out plenty of people who are blessed with such physical gifts who never become great at athletics or, sadly, at anything else in life.

Taken more broadly, I could just as easily talk about having an IQ of 200, or any other superhuman ability that only a few people are ever born with. It's not about what God gave you—not even if you happen to have been born half-dolphin like Michael Phelps, or with the mental horse-power of a savant. It's about how you choose to live your life every day:

- being coachable and hungry to learn;
- being committed to the process of continuous self-improvement;
- believing that you have that special "extra gear" to call on when you really need it, and that win, lose, or draw, you'll rise above fear and self-doubt (your greatest enemies) and give everything you've got, no matter the outcome.

These are the three things you need to be the absolute best, *to be a meaningful force in the universe*—not just in athletics but also in your career, in your relationships, in every single thing you do.

Throughout the rest of this book, I'm going to talk some more about the amazing athletes I've worked with, but remember this: Every quality I describe, every edge that these athletes have—you have them, too.

They are inside you right now. You *know* they are.

So let's find a way to make all those qualities the driving forces in your life.

And you will be closer to unstoppable.

CHAPTER 3

CONTROL THE CONTROLLABLES!

"No one can make you feel inferior without your permission."

From Eleanor Roosevelt, it's one of my favorite quotes of all time.

I once worked for a certain boss who was honestly the most negative, most depressing character I had ever met. He would crack horrible jokes, was always negative and sarcastic, and would scream and curse me out regularly. This man had direct access to my mind for at least twenty hours every week. I was a young man in my early twenties, and I was not equipped to manage the impact he was having on me.

I hated being around him. I hated my job. I hated waking up and going to work. And by the time I was done with my work each day, I would go home miserable, negative, and depressed. And all I could think to do about it was moan and groan and complain to anyone who would listen.

If you happened to be the one listening to me gripe about this guy, and if you tried to convince me that there was something I could do about it—some adjustment in my attitude or in my own thinking—I would have called you a fool or a liar. *He* was the problem, not I. I was trapped, and there was nothing I could do to change things.

Finally, one of my coworkers got tired of hearing me complain. He took me out to lunch, and he shared with me a horror story—the story of my boss's life.

My boss's life was chaos. He was a full-blown chronic alcoholic, so totally controlled by his disease that he had destroyed every meaningful relationship he ever had. He was living in his own personal hell, barely functional, each day worse than the one before—which more than explained his unpredictable and volatile behavior.

Knowing this gave me the chance to see him in a new way. I felt empathy for him, as one human being to another, but at the same time I was able to create an emotional buffer between his life and mine. I no longer internalized his behavior toward me. His mental assaults no longer touched me. This "psychic vampire" had lost his power to drain me of my joy and happiness.

As a young man, I had to learn this painful lesson, but I've shared it many times with others in the years since.

We all have our own fears, our own self-doubts, our own insecurities. They can make us more vulnerable to hostile takeovers, to the psychic vampires all around us, than we care to admit. I'll quote it again, because it's such a simple yet powerful idea:

No one can make you feel inferior without your permission.

One of the greatest challenges I have encountered over the years is getting people to learn how to CONTROL THE CONTROLLABLES. No one in your life can *force* you to feel inferior.

No one!

They can create the conditions that make it more likely you'll feel that way. They can hit the right buttons that have triggered this response from you in the past. They can coerce, persuade, impose, and *insist* that you feel inferior.

But ultimately, it's your choice.

They can't have that power over you unless you *give* it to them.

Now, please know that I'm not talking about extreme circumstances of mental, emotional, and physical abuse. I would never suggest to a battered spouse or an abused child that they can just flip a magic switch in their head and everything will be better. But even in these extreme cases, I've seen firsthand how powerful it can be when a victim reaches that point in their life where they finally reject their victim status and decide in their own heart and mind that they deserve better—and redefine themselves as a survivor.

But for the rest of us, we will have those times when we give coworkers or family members the power to influence the way we feel about ourselves. Ask yourself right now if you need to stop giving someone else in your life this power.

Ultimately, you choose to play the victim and feel trapped and powerless, or you adjust your mindset. To put it another way, you can't control how they treat you. You can't control what they think about you. All you can control is what *you* think about *yourself.*

CONTROL THE CONTROLLABLES. It's one of the central pillars of this whole book—indeed, of everything I talk about to anyone who will listen.

There will be countless other moments in your life when you don't have control over everything around you. Maybe it will be your supervisor or your coach, trying to motivate you by raising their voice and getting under your skin. It's unlikely they'll ever change their style. The only thing that you can change is *your thinking. Your internal reaction.* You can reject taking it personally and focus solely on their intentions, not on their personality. Focus on the objective and the team's or organization's objectives.

That's what *you can control.* Intentionally focus on controlling the controllables.

This idea doesn't apply just to other people who are trying to make you feel a certain way. Think about it—it's life itself! When do you ever have control over *everything*?

Your child is sick. You feel so bad for her. You're overwhelmed. It's natural to feel that way. But think about what you can control in this situation. Can you control what the doctors are doing for her? Or how her body is responding to the medicine?

The one thing you can control is your attitude. Your frame of mind. And most importantly, what you project when you're in the same room with her. Being sad and disheartened—is that in the best interest of your child?

How about being a light of hope for her—the one thing she probably needs right now more than anything else in the world? How about being comforting when she needs to be comforted, and cheering when she needs you to cheer?

That's what you can control.

As I said at the very beginning of this book, this idea of controlling the controllables has never been more important than right now, in this uniquely historic time when we're facing two pandemics at once. One, a viral strand of RNA so small you need an electron microscope to see it, has been with us for just a matter of months. The other is a brutal and systemic form of racial oppression that stretches from one American shore to the other, and it has been with us for over four hundred years.

This is a time that has forced all of us to really face who we are. We're more conscious than ever that there is something new out there that can *kill* us. It's *stalking* us.

I remember an old Richard Pryor record I had, from 1975, and the first routine on it was called "Eulogy." Pryor pretended to be a pastor, standing over a coffin, and this is what he says about the man inside:

> *"He faced the ultimate test, as each man and woman must eventually face the ultimate test. And the ultimate test is, whether or not you can survive death. That's the ultimate test for your ass, ain't it? So far, don't nobody we know have passed the ultimate test."*

That's the ultimate test we've been seeing on television every day, whether it's an emergency room overrun with new patients, or a man held facedown on the pavement with a police officer smugly pressing his knee against the man's neck until he takes his last breath.

In both cases, the imperative is greater than ever to find some way to *stay sane in an insane world*. And this is even more difficult when you've had to shut yourself up in your own house, to live in isolation either alone or with your significant other. (A big challenge either way!)

It's a time where you have to make peace with your own demons, like never before. To take stock of what is working in our lives and what isn't working. To examine our relationships with other people—are they healthy, or unhealthy?

To really take the time to listen to our inner voice.

And then, when we finally have the chance to go back out into the world, how much more important is it to really focus, deliberately and intentionally, on the things that we can change? Or to understand which things we can change *right now* versus the things that will still take more time?

How important is it for us, right now at this moment in history, to make sure that our thoughts and behaviors are consistent with who we want to be in this world?

CONTROL THE CONTROLLABLES. I can't say it enough.

Never forget that you are the only person who has control over your own mind.

REGULATE YOUR
OWN MOODS
INDEPENDENT OF
EXTERNAL FORCES.
—GREG HARDEN

CHAPTER 4

WHO WILL ANSWER?

When Tom Brady came to Michigan, he sure as hell wasn't *Tom Brady* yet. The first two years he was here, he rarely got off the bench. Then—and most people don't even know this—he contracted acute appendicitis and lost twenty-five pounds over the summer. The QB coach who had recruited him was gone by now, and the new QB coach was already unimpressed with Tom's size and athleticism. That opinion didn't get any better when Tom came into the season twenty-five pounds lighter, looking as if he could barely get out of bed, let alone play Big Ten football.

To Tom, it felt as if bad luck had been whipping his butt ever since the day he came to Michigan. He actually thought about transferring back to a school in California. But then he decided to do something else:

He came in to see me.

The Tom Brady I saw in my office was not only underweight, but also discouraged, distressed, and overwhelmed. He had reached his Hamlet moment, the ultimate existential crisis. He didn't know who he was, where he belonged, or why he had come all the way across the country just to sit on the bench and watch the other quarterbacks on the team play.

"The coaches don't believe in me," he said.

I thought about that for a beat. Then I said: "You're right, they don't."

He looked a little surprised. This was *not* the little pep talk he'd been expecting.

"Why should they believe in you," I said, "if you don't believe in yourself?"

Tom could have gotten up and walked out at that point. But he stayed.

"I'm sorry, Tom," I said. "I can't help you become the starter at Michigan. But what I can help you with is this: I can help you *believe* you should be the starter at Michigan."

He kept listening to me.

"If you believe in yourself," I said, "it doesn't matter what anyone else thinks. You've got to believe, whether you are playing, starting, or sitting on the bench, that you are *capable*, you are *qualified*, and you are *confident*."

That was the beginning of my relationship with the young man who would go on to be arguably the greatest quarterback in the history of the NFL. People often ask me these days, "Did you know?" As if there were any way I could have known that he would go on to win seven Super Bowls. But I did know that Tom Brady was determined to do whatever it took to become the best version of himself he could be. And to become the starting quarterback at the University of Michigan.

To his credit, and to the credit of his amazing family, Tom soaked up every drop of advice I gave him. He became obsessed with the mental side of the game. He studied not just offensive plays and strategies, but also defenses. In time, he came to understand all the schemes and tendencies as well as any defensive coordinator in the country. On the physical side, he became that one guy you had to ask to leave the building at the end of the day. "Hey, go home already, get some rest."

But the most impressive thing for me was how Tom trusted me to help him redirect his mind, focus on how to be the best at believing in himself, and be prepared to play quarterback at Michigan. Because Tom knew a very important truth: In the sport of football, *as with anything else in life*, the day will come when you have your opportunity to play. You just have to make sure that your mind, body, and spirit are ready for that day.

Tom's day came at Michigan. He started twenty-five games in 1998 and 1999, going 20-5 with over five thousand yards passing and thirty-five touchdowns. And in the best bowl game performance I've ever seen, he threw four touchdowns in the 2000 Orange Bowl to beat Alabama, bringing the team back from two 14-point deficits.

So when Tom Brady left Michigan, did he start in the NFL and immediately become the best quarterback in the game?

No, he headed straight into another soul-crushing disappointment.

I can still remember the first day of the 2000 NFL draft when Tom was eagerly waiting to hear his name called.

It didn't happen.

I remember talking to him that night, hearing the devastation in his voice. He had to go to bed that night, try to sleep, then get up the next day . . .

Just to keep waiting some more.

The fourth round came and went. Then the fifth round.

It wasn't until the *sixth* round when Tom Brady finally became the 199th player selected in the draft, by the New England Patriots. That's the moment when he could have turned right back into that skinny kid I had first seen in my office, the backup on the bench who didn't think anyone believed in him.

But Tom had a different plan.

On the first day of training camp, he famously told the owner of the Patriots, Robert Kraft, "I'm the best decision this organization has ever made." Then he got to work, using the same mindset he had developed at Michigan, knowing that he would get his opportunity, making sure he was ready when it came. In the second game of his second season, he came in to replace the injured starter and never gave the job back, taking his team all the way to the Super Bowl and becoming the youngest quarterback ever to win it. And then, even as I was writing this book, he led a new team to the 2021 Super Bowl and became the *oldest* quarterback ever to win it!

People talk about luck, but the luck I believe in happens when opportunity knocks on your door and you have already done the work required to make the most of it.

Because here's the problem: If you think that whatever happens to you is just a matter of "good luck" or "bad luck," then whenever you run into an obstacle, you're going to believe that it's out of your control. "I'm just a victim of fate!"

You don't want to be that person.

You want to be the person who sees that obstacle as just another kind of opportunity. You want to believe that the hard work of practicing, training, and rehearsing for success will give you the right mindset to turn troubled times into valuable lessons that get you closer to your goal.

When opportunity and preparation come together, you can do almost anything. Being prepared for opportunity is a lot better than wishing, hoping, betting, or playing the lottery.

Ultimately, you must believe in something larger than luck. You must have the focus to set goals. And you must have the determination to work hard, to be deliberate and intentional in everything you do, so that *you will be prepared when opportunity knocks.*

Opportunity will knock. I guarantee it.

Who will answer?

CHAPTER 5

DREAM BIG, BELIEVE BIG, BECOME BIG

I think I've already started to make the point that the carpet outside my office door has been worn thin by young athletes who were unhappy.

Unhappy with their playing time. Unhappy with how the coaches didn't believe in them. (Remember Tom Brady?) Unhappy with *everything*.

At the end of the 1989 football summer camp, I met one of the unhappiest athletes of all time: a young receiver on the football team, named Desmond Howard.

Most people don't know this, but Desmond was actually a running back in high school. His nickname back then was "Magic," because not only could he run circles around every defender on the football field, his skills on the basketball court were reportedly just as brilliant. That's why they called him "Magic," to acknowledge his hero, the Lakers star Magic Johnson.

But after two years on the Michigan football team, Desmond wasn't feeling so magical. He wasn't even a running back anymore. The coaches had moved him to receiver. So he finally stopped me after summer camp one day and asked if he could talk to me.

What I didn't know that day was that Desmond Howard had been watching me, *studying me* very carefully for over a year, ever since he first set foot on that campus. Today was the day when he had finally decided to take that risk, to confide in me and see what I was all about.

(This may be the perfect spot to let you know that athletes who have *asked* for help tend to have better outcomes than those who are *required* to meet with me.)

When Desmond sat down, the first thing he did was tell me all about the big dreams he had for his football career—big dreams that were not coming true. After a year and a half on the team, Desmond was starting to think that maybe it was time for the old "geographical cure." You know, the belief that if you go to another team (or another place to work, another city to live in), everything will suddenly turn out right. Even though you've changed *nothing* else about yourself, just packing up and moving will somehow magically fix everything.

Desmond asked me quite seriously for my opinion on this idea.

"Right now," I said, "you're telling me how good you are, but I've seen no evidence to support that yet. So at this stage in the game, if you leave, who gives a rat's ass?"

That was the moment. He could have gotten up right then and walked out the door. But he didn't.

"It's July," I said, "which means it's probably too late to catch on with another team, anyway. So if you accept the reality that you're *probably* going to be here at least one more year, I'd use that time to establish that you're the best athlete on the team."

He kept listening.

"If you really believe in yourself," I said, "then there's only one way to change things. You need to start doing everything different. *Everything*. You need to walk different. Talk different. Train different. Play different. And you have to stop caring about what everybody else thinks about you. If a coach believes in you, great! If they don't seem to, then don't get distracted by it. What *you* believe is all that matters."

He was soaking up every word I said. Processing the information like a supercomputer.

"You have to have a single-minded focus," I said. "You have to be assertive. You have to run your own race. You have to give 100 percent, 100 percent of the time, and *believe in yourself.*"

That day marked the beginning of an amazing friendship that would withstand the test of time and a hell of a lot more.

"It's not enough to dream big," I told him. "Big dreams are easy. You gotta *believe* big to *become* big."

So that's what Desmond Howard did. He put his ego aside—not an easy thing for a superbly gifted athlete to do—and he put his trust in me. He believed, without any hesitation, in the formula for success that I was giving him.

But he wanted even more from me. He kept challenging me to help take him to the next level, then the next. I had never met a young man who was so determined to plot, plan, scheme, and ultimately do everything he could to become the absolute best. A young man who could truly step outside himself and look at his own physical, mental, and spiritual strengths and weaknesses. He *demanded* honest feedback and critiques on his every move, both on the field and off. He had this hunger to be the best, to grow, to push himself to break away from everyone else.

I'm telling you this straight: Desmond Howard, at twenty years of age, was the single most relentless individual I had ever met when it came to studying other people's successes and failures, peeling back the layers, and solving the mystery of what works and what doesn't.

He didn't just dream big—he *believed* big, and he learned to be deliberate and intentional about the work he had to do to *become* big.

Desmond was one of the first athletes, and ultimately one of the most successful, at buying into what I considered my most important mission in life: *to teach people how to become the world's greatest experts on themselves.* And Desmond began to believe that his own life was going to be amazing, either with or without football. (Suddenly, football became what he *did* and not who he *was*. He just happened to play it better than most.) Just becoming the best Desmond Howard he could be—that was his obsession.

Desmond would go on to become the best college football player in America, winning the Heisman Trophy in 1991. But fast-forward six more years. Desmond is about to play in Super Bowl XXXI, as a kickoff and punt return specialist for the Green Bay Packers.

It's the night before the game, and I've found my way down to New Orleans because that's a promise Desmond made to me: *If we get to the Super Bowl, you're going to be there.*

I'm in his hotel room, and he's getting ready to play in the biggest game of his life. And he is jacked up, fired up, hyped up, and ready to go.

"I'm going to score a touchdown tomorrow," he said. "Maybe two."

Okay, he's just getting himself psyched up for the game, I thought. I wouldn't have expected anything less.

"We studied them," he said, referring to the New England Patriots they'd be playing the next day. "They don't know how to defend special teams. We're totally going to dominate that phase of the game."

The next day, Desmond Howard set a record for most return yards in a Super Bowl, putting his team in a great position all game, and then scoring the game-clinching touchdown on a ninety-nine-yard kickoff return. He was the first return specialist ever to be named Super Bowl MVP.

I'm telling you about two different days in the life of one man, set six years apart. On that first day, I was asking him to dream big and then to believe big—to believe in *himself*, in his own God-given abilities, and in how far those abilities would take him if he created the right mindset to go with them.

On that second day, six years later, he was dreaming even bigger, believing even bigger—not just in himself this time, but in his *team*. And he was telling *me* about how all the hard work on his mental game was going to be seen by everyone watching the Super Bowl. Wow!

The dream wasn't just an easy pipe dream, and the belief was based on something real—his own hard work and preparation, plus the hard work and preparation of an entire organization around him.

He plotted, planned, schemed, and dreamed, and believed with all his heart that his team was going to put him in a position to tear that place up.

And that's exactly what happened.

After eleven seasons in the NFL, he got an audition to become one of the commentators on ESPN's *College GameDay*. He put just as much hard work and preparation into winning that job, and you can still see him on that program every Saturday morning. He still calls me, still wants my honest feedback, because the hunger is still there to keep growing, to keep improving, and to be the best version of himself.

He's still dreaming big and believing big.

I believe very strongly that there are three levels of fitness: physical, mental, and spiritual. When I say spiritual, I'm not just talking about an organized religion. I'm talking about tapping into something deep within yourself—that inner core, that spirit, that *soul*, if you want to call it that.

The belief I'm talking about in this chapter comes from that place, however you want to define it.

(For Desmond Howard, his confidence was always grounded and enhanced by his faith. In his belief that he was "blessed and highly favored" and that "no weapon formed against him could prosper.")[1]

You've been in a situation where you weren't supposed to get the deal, but somehow you said the right thing, something that came to you out of nowhere. You kicked into that higher gear and you closed the deal.

Or you decided that you weren't going to lose the game and you looked at your teammates and told them, *We're getting ready to turn it up.*

(I talk more about this "extra gear" in "Chapter 2: What Makes Them Different?")

To be able to tap into that source, that part of who you are that transcends thinking—that's what I'm talking about. We've all done it; we've all seen it.

Faith is belief without proof. Something deeper than your own thoughts. Giving your all, win, lose, or draw—that takes some version of faith, whatever that means to you. And sometimes that faith is the only way you're going to win that game, or the only way you're going to get that contract. It's the only way to reach a new level of excellence.

So I ask you: What is your big dream?

More importantly, what do you believe? And what will you become?

1. Isaiah 54:17

DESMOND HOWARD

TESTIMONIAL

Desmond Howard won the Heisman Trophy in 1991, went on to play eleven seasons in the NFL, and was named MVP of Super Bowl XXXI. He is currently an analyst on ESPN's *College GameDay*.

"If Greg Harden isn't at the University of Michigan, I don't win the Heisman."

It's hard to put into words all the things that Greg has taught me. But I think he helped me, and a lot of other people, to see the big picture. He teaches you to see beyond yourself. But at the same time, to look *within* yourself. To tap into the greatness that's inside you.

It takes a true *selflessness* to be able to do that. To be honest with yourself in terms of what's working in your life and what's *not* working.

Greg's basic lesson has always been about avoiding self-defeating attitudes and behaviors, and that's something I've carried with me throughout my whole life, in any job, any situation, any predicament I've ever found myself in.

Another basic lesson is the importance of *preparation*. It's part of seeing the bigger picture. Looking beyond just the next game. He told me, "Don't just be the best football player. Be the most dominant, best *athlete* on the field. Think like, train like, and *become* like an Olympic athlete. If you think and behave that way, you will separate yourself from all of the other players on the team."

So that's what I trained myself to do. It takes a certain amount of commitment and dedication in order to execute that level of preparation. It's not just physical—in fact, it's much more mental than physical, because you have to mentally prepare yourself if you're going to be able to do everything you're calling on yourself to do.

I've taken the same idea, the same commitment to mental preparation, and I've applied it in everything I've done in my life after football. Everything I do, I use the same life lessons I learned from Greg.

No matter what you do—whatever sport, whatever job, whatever part of your life—you should always want to get better at it. Never get content with where you are. Never rest on your laurels. Never settle for "good enough."

Sometimes, that means finding someone that you really respect, someone who will be truthful with you and give you honest feedback. If you can find someone like that in your life, it's a real blessing!

For me, everything starts with attitude. If you don't have the right attitude, your behavior is going to follow suit, and you'll never be able to perform at a high level. Not just in athletics. It goes way beyond that. Academically, socially, it's all about controlling your own mindset.

The way you see yourself, and the way you see the situations around you every day—that's going to control everything. If it's not working, then you have to start seeing things through a different lens, a different perspective.

Because in the end, no matter what you do, it's not about talent.

It's about what's going on inside your own head!

HUMAN BEINGS ARE THE ONLY CREATURES WITH THE ABILITY TO DECIDE THEY'RE NOT GOING TO BE THE SAME TODAY AS THEY WERE YESTERDAY.

—GREG HARDEN

CHAPTER 6:

WHAT DOES SUCCESS LOOK LIKE?

I met Michael Phelps in 2004. He was nineteen years old, and he had just come home from the Olympics in Athens, with six gold medals and two bronze. His longtime coach, Bob Bowman, had just accepted the job as the new swimming coach for the University of Michigan. In fact, I had helped make that hire happen, and I oversaw the swim program as its sports administrator—with no clue about what would happen next. Phelps followed Bowman to Ann Arbor, served as a volunteer assistant coach for the swim team, and began training in the Michigan pool for the 2008 Olympics in Beijing.

Now, understand that Phelps was *not* an official Michigan student athlete. It was an unusual situation, but who's going to turn down the chance to have an Olympic champion help train your swim team?

Bob and I had a great relationship. I talked to him often. He confided in me that coaching Michael Phelps was the biggest challenge of his career. He had started training him full-time when he was eleven years old—*eleven!*—and had taken Michael as a fifteen-year-old to the 2000 Olympics in Sydney, where he finished fifth in the 200-meter butterfly. Now he was nineteen years old, fresh off his second trip to the Olympics, and wearing six gold and two bronze medals around his neck. Michael had been training with Bob for eight years at that point—the best swimmer in America, with a chance to become the best *ever*.

But the relationship between coach and swimmer was not good.

Michael was becoming moodier, more defiant, and openly rebellious about his training schedule. The previous fall, he had been arrested in Maryland for driving under the influence of alcohol, had pleaded guilty, and was still serving his eighteen months of probation.

Bob was eager for me to work with Michael. But I knew I couldn't force the issue—it had to be Michael's idea to talk to me. Or at least, it had to *feel* that way. So I told Bob to let Michael know I was available and then to let natural human curiosity take over.

A few days later, Michael showed up at my door.

"I think I understand what you're going through," I said to him.

He looked surprised.

"You've been training since you were eleven years old," I went on. "You never really had a childhood."

I knew that his parents had been divorced for most of his life. He had spent most of his time training with Bob, first in Maryland, now in Michigan. When other teenagers were playing video games, going out on dates, or just hanging out at the mall, Michael's whole life was centered on the time he spent swimming from one end of a pool to the other.

"It's natural that you'd need to rebel a little bit," I said. "And who else but Bob, the central parent figure in your life, are you gonna rebel against?"

I let Michael think about that. I could tell it was ringing true with him. I had started to win his trust, had shown him that I understood where he was coming from. We kept talking on a regular basis, until it was time for me to shift the tone of my message. I challenged him to think about what he really wanted out of his life. Because he could walk away from the sport right then with eight Olympic medals, six of them gold—an achievement most people could only dream about. To anyone else, his life already was a success.

But not to himself.

That's the one thing I knew about Michael Phelps. Everything else aside, this young man had a passion for swimming—a burning competitive drive that could propel him to unprecedented heights in his sport.

"As good as you are," I told him, "we still don't know how good you can be. You still haven't given 100 percent, 100 percent of the time."

It was insanity to be saying this to an athlete who spent his whole life training, who had already proved himself one of the best swimmers in the world. But he didn't argue with me.

"God knows what it would be like," I said, "if you actually stopped rebelling and started giving 100 percent."

I'm not claiming that just a few meetings with Michael Phelps turned his life around. But I know I got through to him. I know I got him thinking that day about his own goals and what he really wanted to achieve in his life. As I think everyone knows at this point, Michael went to the 2008 Olympics in Beijing and won a record eight gold medals. He would go on to become the greatest swimmer and most decorated Olympian ever, with a record twenty-eight medals, twenty-three of them gold. Just as importantly, he's been on his own personal mission ever since leaving the sport, speaking out at every opportunity about his own mental health issues and helping everyone around him to know that it's "okay not to be okay" sometimes, and that we *all* reach points in our life when we need to seek help.

Looking back on everything that Michael Phelps has done, I'm going to go ahead and call his life a success. He has an amazing family, he is an exceptional businessman, and his commitment to promoting mental-health awareness is a true game changer.

This is a question I've asked thousands of other people over the years, in seminars and workshops, and I'll ask it to you right now: What does success look like for you?

The first answers I get are usually predictable. Money, power, fame.

I never think those answers are enough. Because they're too easy, and half the time they're just the answers we've been programmed to give. If I have money, if I have power, if I have fame, then I'll be successful. Then I'll be happy.

I ask them to go deeper. To describe, in vivid detail, *their own personal definition of success*. How success would feel to them, how it would sound, how it would smell, how it would taste.

When people have the opportunity to really think about it, the answers I've gotten back have been a lot more meaningful. A successful life becomes a matter of meeting your own personal goals for yourself—and the motivation and energy to achieve those goals must be drawn from a deeper source than the outward expectations of others, or the siren song of corporate advertising. It has to come from your own soul.

When you're following the right path in your life, you immediately feel at peace with its direction. That's how you *know* you're on the right path. Your heart, your mind, your spirit—they all tell you.

The goals that you have for your life serve as the compass points as you walk that path. Meeting each of those goals becomes a measure of your progress, and as long as those goals stay aligned with your deeper purpose, each one will result in greater success. This is the essential relationship between your goals and your purpose in life. One without the other is meaningless.

I've met plenty of people who seem totally "goal-oriented," but their goals are driven by the expectations of others and not connected to their deeper purpose. These people are always focused on getting stuff done, but is it the *right* stuff? Are they putting their energy in the direction of the things that will make their lives more meaningful and fulfilling? As Stephen Covey highlights in *The 7 Habits of Highly Effective People*, purpose is what should drive everything. It's impossible to be a truly effective, productive, fulfilled person without first understanding your *purpose* and aligning your goals with that purpose.

Before we go any further, I want you to take a moment to think about the purpose of your life. Nobody else's life, just yours. It may not come as a great revelation or a burning bush in the wilderness. For most of us, it unfolds like a well-told story, coming into clear focus only over time. The key is to listen to yourself and to get in tune with your inner voice.

What is your purpose?

And then, building on that, *what is your own personal definition of success?*

Let's step back and ask a more basic question: *Where does the motivation to achieve success come from?* Even if we've clearly defined our own version of success for ourselves, from where do we draw the motivation to consistently set goals and then do the hard work to achieve them?

Beyond our basic biological needs for food, shelter, and safety, I contend that our *emotional needs* are the strongest drivers of our behaviors. I also contend that we all have the basic right to have our emotional needs met. *The key is to make sure that the way in which we satisfy our emotional needs is in tune with our goals, not in conflict.*

In the same seminars and workshops where I've asked the participants to consider their own definition of success, I've also introduced this idea of how we meet our emotional needs. I ask a very simple question:

"What do you think all people need to have in order to make their lives work?"

The responses I've received over the years can be narrowed down to a consistent set of emotional needs that some people call "the four A's":

Attention. We all need attention, at the very least from our friends and loved ones. The lack of attention is isolation, and prolonged isolation causes one to become depressed and withdrawn. This basic need for attention is most pronounced in children. The attention of parents and other caring adults is absolutely required for normal emotional and mental development.

Of course, some people can develop a counterproductive dependence on attention from others, to the point that they act out in irrational ways just to receive that attention—even if it's negative.

Ultimately, you can take it all the way down to a basic existential level: *One way or another, you're going to know I exist.*

Affection. Every psych student knows the experiment with the young monkeys who were provided with two kinds of artificial "mothers." The first was a cold wire cage that dispensed food; the second was covered with sheepskin and a light bulb, to provide the monkey with a minimal level of "affection." The monkeys went to the wire-cage mother only when they needed food. For every other minute of their confinement, they clung to the sheepskin mother. Clearly, it was the latter that gave the monkeys the affection they needed more than food.

Even more dramatically, the group of young monkeys that were given the same amount of food but no affection at all—not even something as artificial as a sheepskin and a light bulb—became severely stunted. Their brains, spines, and internal organs never developed to full size.

Tragically, we see this phenomenon play out all around us. Children who grow up without real affection become emotionally arrested, dysfunctional adults.

Affection isn't just a nice, warm, fuzzy thing that we get to have in our lives if we're lucky. It is as essential to us as food and water.

Approval. We like to think of ourselves as independent human beings, but face it—the need for approval is one of the strongest driving forces in the world. This need is particularly acute when we're children. But consider how *approval* can often become just another term for *conditional love*: I'll be so proud of you if you get all A's. If you behave. If you clean your room. Or for a father especially: If you catch the ball, run the 100, make the basket . . .

Again, this need can manifest in unhealthy ways if the approval given is based on *too many* conditions or if the conditions are all but impossible to meet. How many addicts and alcoholics, how many young suicide attempts, can be traced back to a need for approval that was never met?

Acceptance. I put this one last for a reason. While *approval* is often based on conditional love, *acceptance* is truly unconditional. (For more on this idea, see "Chapter 16. The Two Kinds of Love.") It's a motherly kind of love, a God-like love. An acceptance of who you are, no matter what you do, no matter what mistakes you've made in your life. Or, just as importantly, if you've made no mistakes at all but are just *different.* You may not conform to a preconceived notion of what you should be, how you should look, who you should love. Ultimately, self-acceptance is crucial, and it will protect you from "should" and "ought to."

We all seek acceptance from our parents and other loved ones. Or from society as a whole. If we can't get it, we'll often do whatever we must to get approval. We all want acceptance. Sometimes, we settle for approval.

Let's tie this all together. I asked you to think hard about your own purpose in life, and what success would really look like *for you*. Once you understand that, you can set the ideal goals for your life.

As you think about this, keep the four A's in mind, because it's essential to understand your motivations. *Because your motivations, the human desire to satisfy those basic emotional needs, are the keys to understanding which of your attitudes and behaviors are helping you achieve your goals—and which ones are holding you back.*

Please remember these things as you go to the next chapter!

(Note: I encourage you to start filling out the "Worksheet: My Purpose, My Goals, My SDABs and SSABs" on page 56, and to keep this with you through the next two chapters.)

CHAPTER 7:

THE DEMON ON YOUR LEFT SHOULDER:
Self-*Defeating* Attitudes and Behaviors

Okay, I confess: I was thinking of giving this chapter a title like, "The Funnest Damn Chapter in the Whole Book," just to make sure that you don't skip it. But I'll be straight with you and assume you got here the right way—particularly if you read "Chapter 6: What Does Success Look Like?"—and are now following through to the next topic. (In fact, if you haven't read the previous chapter yet, please back up and do so right now!)

The thread we're following here is that once you've identified your current purpose in life and then defined your personal version of success, you need to set *actionable goals* that will become like landmarks on that road. At the same time, I asked you to consider the emotional needs that we all have. I identified them as the four A's: attention, affection, approval, and acceptance—all as essential to our well-being as food, shelter, and safety. I then asked you to consider how we can satisfy these emotional needs (as we all must), in a way that is *in tune* with our goals, not in conflict. In a way that keeps us on the right road to success instead of leading us into the ditch.

One of the most memorable people ever to sit in my office chair was a woman named Eva Cole. She had just come to America from mainland China, and her stories of her young life spent there would curl the hair on your neck and arms.

She had been through much trauma as a female in a very traditional Chinese family. She had rebelled against the strictly defined role forced upon her and was severely chastised by her brothers and her sisters as well for many of the decisions she made. She finally left it all behind and came to America.

Eva was a powerfully motivated person—to get this far in her life, she had to be. And she was a great friend to everyone around her, and a great mother to her kids. By any measure, she had built a great new life.

Unfortunately, she still carried some emotional wounds that had never healed. She was still haunted by her experiences in China, and these would sometimes threaten to drown her in an all-consuming, overwhelming sadness.

I had been working with her for months, trying to train her to listen to how she talked to herself, and teaching her different methods of reframing and reinterpreting these childhood experiences now that she was an adult. But we had hit a wall.

I was about to suggest that she move on to another professional, someone who might have a more effective approach to helping her deal with her anxiety. But then I decided to try one more thing.

Did I mention, by the way, that Eva stood about five foot three and weighed basically nothing? That's what made my decision so radical: because this exercise I wanted to suggest was something I generally saved for male athletes who spend much of their time in the weight room.

I asked her to keep talking about the events from her past, but this time I wanted her to stand while doing it.

She looked at me a little funny, but she agreed. She stood up and kept talking about how she never felt happy with her life, never received approval from her family.

A minute later, I interrupted her.

"Are you strong enough to lift that chair you were sitting in?"

She looked at me funny again, looked back at the chair, shrugged her shoulders, and said, "Of course I am."

"So pick it up," I said. "And keep talking."

She picked up the chair and kept talking. More woe and misfortune followed, until I stopped her one more time.

"Are you strong enough to lift that chair over your head?"

She was a proud woman who had never backed down from anything. So of course she said, "Yes."

She lifted the chair over her head. I told her to keep talking. And she did. She never missed a beat, just kept on lamenting how she felt demeaned and put down for her efforts to be assertive and forward-thinking.

I let her go on for a couple of minutes, until I started to see her arms shake. "Eva," I said, "is that chair getting heavy?"

"No," she said, "I can hold it."

"Okay, then continue."

She went on with her story, telling me how, no matter how successful she was in raising her children, starting successful businesses, and helping and encouraging others, she still felt trapped, still struggled to see herself as worthy and valued. I kept stopping her every two minutes as I listened, asking her if she was uncomfortable yet. She kept shaking me off, told me she was fine.

Until finally, it was too much for her.

She put the chair down with a heavy clunk and looked me in the eye. "This is ridiculous. Why are you making me do this?"

"That chair is yesterday's baggage," I said. "You've been dragging it around for your entire adult life—every place you've been, every relationship. Aren't you getting tired of carrying this baggage everywhere you go?"

This session with Eva was not the first time I had seen someone sabotage their own life and successes with a particular attitude or behavior. Over the years, I've been helping people identify these attitudes and behaviors as the first step to dealing with them. I've been calling them "self-defeating attitudes and behaviors" ever since—sometimes "SDABs" for short. If you're in the people-helping business, or if you just have a keen eye for human psychology in action, you've seen these kinds of attitudes and behaviors before: There's the talented athlete who sabotages her own success—not to mention her *team's* success—through a basic inability to get along with others. And how about the academically gifted student who has to pretend not to care about school so his peers will see him as "cool."

Sometimes, these attitudes and behaviors are glaringly obvious. Sometimes, they're masked and almost impossible to see, as in someone with a deeply ingrained "fear of success," who derails his or her own life in cleverly disguised ways. But no matter how recognizable these attitudes and behaviors are, they will always be much easier to see in someone else than in ourselves. This is why self-honesty is so essential for this kind of work.

The first key point to remember is that we all sometimes encounter emotions, or find ourselves engaging in behaviors, that defeat our higher selves, that undermine our highest ambitions for who we are and who we aspire to be.

The second key point is that we all have the power to *reinterpret* our experiences, to *redefine* ourselves, to *reinvent* ourselves, and to *readjust* our attitudes and behaviors.

As you think about the self-defeating attitudes and behaviors that may be standing in the way of you reaching your own goals—thereby preventing you from attaining your own definition of success and fulfilling your own purpose in life—please consider some of these "usual suspects" that I've seen countless times in my career as a counselor:

REFUSING TO RELINQUISH YESTERDAY'S BAGGAGE

Remember Eva holding the chair over her head. More generally, the "baggage" is the heavy burden we can carry when we can't get over past events, assaults, insults, trauma—*anything* from our past.

- *My dad never showed me he loved me; therefore, I am not lovable.*
- *My siblings always got treated better than I, so I don't want them in my life, because they are a source of pain and bad memories.*
- *I've seen people mistake kindness for weakness, so I have to be extremely aggressive to feel respected and safe.*
- *Every time I trust somebody, they hurt me, so I'm just not going to trust anybody ever again.*

When we hold on to yesterday's negative experiences or unfinished business, we're essentially living in a mental time warp, always trying to relive and correct the past. With no resolution, we struggle to move forward.

SELF-DOUBT

We all doubt our own abilities, worthiness, or value at one time or another, but chronic self-doubt can be debilitating. The roots often trace back to experiences in our upbringing. As children, we may have been conditioned by something or someone to believe negative things about ourselves. It undermines our happiness and puts us constantly at war with ourselves. When we doubt ourselves, we *reject* compliments and positive feedback and always question how others perceive us.

OVERGENERALIZING

These are the beliefs, usually learned at a young age, that limit the way we see the world around us, and hurt our relationships with others.

- *I believe that women are stupid.*
- *I believe that men cannot be trusted.*
- *I believe that members of this particular race are inferior.*

Beliefs like these prevent us from growing as individuals, and severely limit our understanding of the world. The longer we cling to them, the more bitter and more negative we will become, refusing to see any reality that contradicts our precious limiting beliefs.

REFUSING TO ASK FOR HELP

One of my father's favorite sayings was, "If you see me in a bear fight, don't help me, help the bear!" As a young child, I internalized this deeply, and it only grew stronger as I grew up in a world that seemed to put a high value on self-reliance and rugged individualism. But *never* asking for help can actually disguise a profound insecurity: a belief that needing help is a sign of weakness, and a false sense of superiority thinking that nobody around you could help you, anyway. In time, this attitude will *always* end up hurting you in the workplace, at school, as part of your team on the athletic field, and in all your relationships.

One of the best moments in my adult life came when I got a call from my father (not a common occurrence in itself). We chatted for a while about sports and politics, until finally he said to me, "The reason I'm calling is to get some advice from you. I need your help." What a wonderful moment that was, and what a major breakthrough for us in beginning a new relationship!

REFUSING TO ADMIT THAT YOU'RE WRONG

This is a big one for so many people! As in "refusing to ask for help," it is a fake strength hiding a very real weakness. I'm going to admit right here that I've been guilty of this one myself, more times than I care to admit. I'm right in the middle of an argument with my wife, and it dawns on me: *She's right!* That's where the argument should end, but often it doesn't. It's not even about right and wrong anymore, because now I'm just too committed to winning the debate. Does that sound familiar?

I've had to learn that being right is not all it's cracked up to be. In couples counseling, I will pose these questions: What is your objective in coming to see me? Is it to prove who is right? Or is it to be more effective in your relationship?

OBSESSING OVER CRITICISM

Early in my career, I gave a presentation to all the students in a middle school. When it was done, I stayed to talk with a hundred of them. Ninety-eight of those students told me my presentation was great. Two told me it stunk. Can you guess which feedback I obsessed over for days? How can we so easily dismiss and deflect praise in one moment, but then embrace and even obsess over criticism in the next? By the second week, I became aware of my self-defeating attitude and behavior and caught myself in this pattern of craving approval. I reminded myself that 98 percent is not a bad grade! And I stopped dwelling on the other 2 percent.

HOLDING ON TO UNHEALTHY RELATIONSHIPS

Some relationships are built on virtually nothing but pain and unhappiness. Neither party is happy, but both are committed to their shared dysfunction. This could be because they've never known what a truly healthy relationship even looks like. Or maybe one or both parties don't value themselves—don't believe they deserve anything better—and they cling to the idea that even an unhealthy relationship is better than being alone!

Your ability to distinguish the difference between a healthy and an unhealthy relationship may be more valuable than I can even express. And if you cannot free yourself from an unhealthy relationship, please ask for help.

NEGATIVE SELF-TALK

Negative self-talk is the constant stream of destructive fuel we can feed ourselves, convincing ourselves every day that we should always expect the worst. It can sound a lot like this:

- *I am incapable of being happy.*
- *I am not worthy of success.*
- *The challenges in front of me are too great to overcome.*
- *My personality is what it is, and there is no changing me.*
- *I always get less than what I expect.*
- *I suck. And my life sucks.*
- *I can't . . . (fill in the blank).*

It can be more than just a habit, more like a *ritual.* It can be passed down from the people who raise us—essentially an inner "oral tradition" that persists from one generation to the next. Sometimes, it's inserted into our brains by the world (advertising, media, popular culture) all around us. And sometimes, we just create it ourselves because it's familiar, like some perverse sort of comfort food. *(If I cultivate the negative and always expect the worst, I'll never be disappointed.)*

I've worked with many people who rely on negative self-talk to protect themselves from disappointment. If their expectations aren't high, then failure, loss, or other negative results will hurt less.

There are plenty of other self-defeating attitudes and behaviors we could describe here. I've gathered many of them through the interactions I've had in my workshops. Here are just a few:

BLAMING OTHERS

HATING

ACTING INFERIOR

LOSING YOUR TEMPER

BEING LATE

COMPLAINING

COMPARING YOURSELF TO OTHERS

DISTRUSTING OTHERS

PROCRASTINATION

WASTING MONEY

ABUSING OTHERS

CLINGING TO DEPRESSION

STEALING

MAKING EXCUSES

IGNORING THE TRUTH

BEING RECLUSIVE

BEING REVENGEFUL

LYING

GIVING UP WITHOUT TRYING

BEING ARGUMENTATIVE

AVOIDING RESPONSIBILITY

SPREADING RUMORS

FIGHTING

NOT STUDYING

ALWAYS FEELING GUILTY

ACTING DUMB

BEING ARROGANT

NEVER SHARING YOUR TRUE FEELINGS

PUSHING OTHERS AWAY

As someone who has worked for years with people who abuse drugs and alcohol, I'll add one final item to the list:

ADDICTION

I understand the psychology and physiology of addiction, and I can safely say that it is every bit as strong a destructive force as anything else we've talked about here. It could be an addiction to drugs, alcohol, sex, gambling, or any number of compulsive vices. And addiction perfectly illustrates why we, as fallible human beings, can fall prey to any of the self-defeating attitudes and behaviors described in this chapter:

Let's go back to the emotional needs we talked about in these last chapters. The four A's: attention, affection, approval, and acceptance. *The power of self-defeating attitudes and behaviors—the reason we can cling to them so strongly—is because we're trying to satisfy those emotional needs, but in the wrong way.*

Just think about that for a moment! Understand the power of something that satisfies our emotional needs—something as essential to us as food, shelter, and safety—even if it is ultimately destructive to our own success.

Understand that power, and then take another moment to *forgive* yourself for letting yourself be seduced by the false promises that these self-defeating attitudes and behaviors give us.

Now you're ready for the hard part: Identify the three self-defeating attitudes and behaviors that most accurately apply to you and to your life. Take the time to really *think* about this, and honestly face those demons that most often sit on your left shoulder. And don't limit your thinking to the list I've shared here. Add your own ideas on what could be sabotaging your growth.

Now let's talk about the angel on your *other* shoulder.

CHAPTER 8:

THE ANGEL ON YOUR RIGHT SHOULDER:
Self-*Supporting* Attitudes and Behaviors

In the last chapter, we talked about the self-defeating attitudes and behaviors that undermine our highest ambitions for who we are and who we aspire to be. I challenged you to take an honest look at yourself and to identify the specific SDABs that have been holding you back.

Then I asked you to take another moment to *forgive* yourself for allowing yourself to be seduced by these SDABs. You are a human being. You have real emotional needs that are just as essential to you as food, shelter, and safety, and the power behind these SDABs is that they *promise* to fulfill those needs. That promise is a lie, but you aren't the first person to fall for that lie, and you won't be the last.

Now that you've faced the demon that sits on your left shoulder, allow me to continue the cartoon analogy and examine something a lot more uplifting: the *angel* that sits on your right shoulder. The self-supporting attitudes and behaviors that not only fulfill your emotional needs in a healthy way but also help you achieve the goals in your life and truly realize your full potential as a human being.

Remember the four A's—attention, affection, approval, and acceptance—that represent our basic emotional needs? You will find one simple and tremendously powerful idea that runs throughout this whole chapter as we talk about self-supporting attitudes and behaviors.

Simply put the word "self" in front of each of the four A's:

SELF-ATTENTION   SELF-AFFECTION
SELF-APPROVAL   SELF-ACCEPTANCE

Think about it! When you give *yourself* the attention, affection, approval, and acceptance that you need, you *liberate* yourself from the yoke of other people's expectations. You liberate yourself. You empower yourself. And you *free* yourself from all those situations in your life where you're forced to compromise your own happiness—or even your safety and sanity—to get those basic needs met.

When I was thirty years old, I was in my career as a clinical therapist at a drug and alcohol rehabilitation center. It was a great job with great benefits, but more importantly, it was my first real opportunity to practice the craft I had chosen as my life's work. As a young African American man, I would be working predominantly with men who were rooted in the culture of rural Appalachia. I knew I would have to overcome the inevitable social barriers and quickly earn their trust and respect. Without that, I wouldn't be able to accomplish anything.

I believed that I had the skill and the confidence to meet this challenge, but as I started planning for my first sessions, I couldn't shake a nagging sense of anxiety. I knew I had the right training, the right credentials, the right experience for this job, but I couldn't shake the negative self-talk in my head:

- *You don't know what you're doing.*
- *These men are all racists and haters, and they'll never listen to you.*
- *You're going to fail in this job. Everything you've worked for is going to go down the drain.*

This negative self-talk going on inside my head was frankly starting to piss me off. So I asked myself, *What would you tell someone else who is struggling with the same problem?*

Now, this is going to sound a little crazy, but I swear it's true. All this was going on right when Ash Wednesday was just around the corner. I'd heard people talking about giving up something for Lent, but I figured that was a Catholic thing and thus didn't apply to me. But all of a sudden, the idea started to make sense. And I thought to myself, *Why can't I give up fear and self-doubt for Lent?*

So that is what I did—or, at least, tried. I knew it could never be as simple as not eating chocolate for six weeks, but I deliberately and intentionally committed myself to the idea of refusing to entertain thoughts of fear and self-doubt. To do that, I really had to think about where my fear and self-doubt came from in the first place. And a big part of it, I realized, went back to my father.

I know I'm not the only one who's had this kind of experience, but my father was a certain kind of man, from an era when men didn't express themselves emotionally—not to anybody, even their own kids. Those four A's I needed so badly—attention, affection, approval, and acceptance— were not being given to me by my father. Or at least, that's how it *felt* at the time.

But of course, feelings are not facts. As I looked back over my life, I made the conscious decision to see things more clearly and to decide for myself, once and for all, that my father loved me. A simple idea, just those four words. But it meant everything to me.

My father loved me. He just didn't know how to say it.

He was proud of me. He *approved* of me and everything I had accomplished to get to this point in my life, even if he didn't know how to express it.

So now, all these years later, it was time for me to forgive him. I gave up all the resentment I held for the things he hadn't done.

I had to forgive my father for not being perfect.

What a huge weight this lifted from my shoulders. I let go of all this baggage I had with my father, and the voices of fear and self-doubt inside my head quickly got a lot quieter.

I remember the day I had this epiphany—because less than forty-eight hours later, my phone rang. It was my father. (I mentioned this moment when I was describing "Refusing to Ask for Help" in the previous chapter.)

"I need your advice on something," my dad said.

Picture me looking at the phone, thinking, *Who is this?*

"It's a personal thing," he went on. "You know more about this than I do."

Understand, this is the man who thought he knew *everything*. I had never heard him talk this way to anybody, let alone to his own son. For this to happen forty-eight hours after I essentially forgave him for not being the perfect father, it was as if God was giving me an affirmation. Once I let go of my past grievances and *believed* that my father loved me, I was given this amazing gift: concrete proof that I was right.

As great as this moment was for me, I needed to take it even a step further:

> *My father loves me.*
> *God loves me.*
> And most importantly of all: *I love myself.*

I love myself, and I am already capable of meeting any new challenges in my life, and I will continue to be capable—*with or without* anyone else's approval.

That's what it all boils down to! Self-attention, self-affection, self-approval, self-acceptance—all the things that help turn self-defeating attitudes and behaviors into self-*supporting* attitudes and behaviors—are all pieces of a greater whole:

SELF-LOVE

What is love, after all? To love someone is to admire, encourage, support, protect, plan for, look beyond the faults of, focus on the needs of, forgive (because you do not want anything to diminish the love), give attention to, look after, instruct, and not give up on. To love someone is to do all these things.

And to love yourself is to do all these things for yourself.

If you go through life denying yourself this love, what happens? You undervalue yourself, you esteem the qualities of other people instead of your own, you criticize yourself, you see only your mistakes and short-comings, you see everything in your life in a negative light, and you spend all your time and energy trying to make yourself better, hoping against hope that one day you'll be able to accept yourself.

You become your own worst enemy.

But when you finally allow yourself to love yourself, amazing things happen. First of all, by loving ourselves, we become much better at loving others.

But it's not easy, I know! You can't turn around a lifetime of self-hatred in a moment. Some of us were raised in environments where self-love was never modeled for us. We never saw it. So we were programmed to hate ourselves.

This is where the power of choice and free will becomes so important. You have to make a decision to start loving yourself. You have to be *deliberate* and *intentional* about it. You have to make this a project in your life. Something you will *commit* to working on every day.

Sometimes, I have to come right out and tell someone: *Start by being selfish.* (I mean "selfish" in the most positive sense of the word.) It goes against everything you've been taught in your life. But recognizing your own needs in life and valuing them is one essential step toward true self-love.

I was once invited to give a talk to a group of women. My working title for the speech was "One Is a Whole Number," because I wanted to emphasize that no single person should ever feel incomplete. In fact, a sense of self-sufficiency is an absolute necessity *before* entering into a relationship, or else that relationship will be doomed from the start.

But then I had a better idea. Something that would hit them right between the eyes. I changed the title to "You Want Me to Love You, but You Don't Even Like Yourself!" I still laugh remembering the moment I put those words up on the screen, but the words are still sadly appropriate for too many people in this world, single or partnered, young or old.

We all need to love ourselves first before we can truly love anyone else. And self-love is simply recognizing our own inherent worth and value and being willing to invest in ourselves, nurture ourselves, take care of ourselves every day.

Of course, while you're loving yourself, you need to remember to be *real* with yourself, to motivate yourself to become a better person. That's where many of the other self-supporting attitudes and behaviors come into play. I'll list a few of them here:

LETTING GO OF YESTERDAY'S BAGGAGE AND FORGIVING

Remember Eva Cole from the previous chapter, who I asked to hold a chair over her head to represent all the unresolved trauma she was still carrying around every day of her life? If you're anything like her, what a relief it would be to finally resolve that trauma and let go of that baggage! But how do you know if you've really done this? Here are three reliable signs:

1. You can talk about the experience without returning to that original emotional state you felt when it happened.
2. You can clearly articulate how you made sense of what happened to you, and how you overcame it.
3. You can identify how dealing with this experience has made you a better, stronger, more resilient person.

Often, the baggage I see people carrying comes from not being able to forgive their parents for how they raised them, and for specific instances of trauma they caused in their young child's life. *For me, one of the biggest keys to sound mental health is being able to forgive your parents for being less than perfect.* It's not easy, but forgiving your parents will free you and heal you in ways you probably can't even imagine. If you're struggling with this, I want you to remember something vitally important: If you can't forgive your parents for *their* sake, then do it for *yours*.

TAKING RESPONSIBILITY FOR YOURSELF

As you're thinking about any of these potential changes in your life, the best way to completely lose your steam is to see your own circumstances and your own state of mind as something outside your control. If you really believe that, then you'll never believe you can change anything!

I'm telling you right now, your life belongs to you, and it is your responsibility to make the most of it. Nobody else can do this for you. Not I, not your spouse, not your parents, not your children, not your friends. Taking responsibility for your own life—making your own life's outcome your highest priority—is the essential groundwork for *any* positive change in your life.

ASKING FOR HELP

Yes, it's your life and your responsibility, but that doesn't mean you can't ask for help when you really need it. Too many of us are trained from an early age to consider asking for help a sign of weakness. But here's something important to realize: many of the most successful businesspeople, entertainers, and just regular people enjoying great lives were able to achieve their success by accepting help from someone else at some key point in their life. If you want to become more comfortable with the idea of being able to ask for help, I suggest doing three things:

1. Read or watch a biography of someone you really admire. If you delve deeply enough into the life of any great man or woman, you're all but certain to find that they allowed someone to help them at one time or another. (Martin Luther King, Jr., Helen Keller, Bill Gates, Michael Jordan . . . I could go on for days.) It was okay for them to ask, and it's okay for you, just as you will be asked to help someone else someday.

2. Once you've decided that you will ask for help, you need to identify the times when you really need it. Now, if you start going around asking people for money or other material things, you know that those people will start to avoid you or view you with suspicion. I'm talking about asking someone for advice, for support, for direction. Those are more valuable than the material things, anyway, and probably what you really need help with.

3. Finally, be clear on what you're really asking for. Take the time to sort out what you actually need in your life. In fact, write it down. That way, you'll be clear when you articulate what you need.

LETTING YOUR EGO *HELP* YOU INSTEAD OF JUST *INFLATE* YOU

This isn't the most obvious thing to include on a list like this, but I *love* the idea of making your ego your best friend. When used in the right way, your ego can really drive you whenever you need to respond to a challenge in your life. If that challenge is simply to become a better person and to do the hard work to make that happen, your ego can be the engine that gets you there. I've seen this so many times working with top athletes. Tom Brady used his ego in a positive way to endure all the rigorous training, ignore all the doubters, and ultimately become the best quarterback who ever played the game. And he's *still* not satisfied. *The secret is to make your ego your ally, not your enemy.*

SURROUNDING YOURSELF WITH QUALITY PEOPLE

Human beings are social creatures. We're inevitably influenced by the people around us, at every stage in life. The way we talk, the way we walk, even the car we drive. So, since we know we're going to be influenced, why not resolve to surround ourselves with quality people—the kind of people who will reinforce the positive attributes and behaviors in your life, instead of the negative? But please remember that this usually doesn't happen by accident. You have to search for these quality people around you. You have to *recruit* them into your life. And, of course, the best way to meet these quality people in the first place is to start *becoming* one yourself.

As you can see, there's no secret code here. You can look at any of the self-defeating attitudes and behaviors in the previous chapter and consider the direct opposite—the self-*supporting* attitude and behavior that undoes the damage done by that SDAB and puts things right in your life. Here are few more, and I'll bet you could add some of your own:

- Reaffirming past accomplishments
- Redirecting negative self-talk
- Committing to overcome fears and self-doubt
- Rewarding yourself in healthy ways
- Creating and using support groups

- Adapting to change
- Being supportive and trusting of others
- Routinely examining your circle of friends
- Being as attentive to yourself as you are to others
- Being as affectionate to yourself as you are to others
- Using conflict to promote positive change
- Taking charge of your mental, physical, and spiritual health
- Mastering relationships with people, places, and things
- Being a participant as well as an observer

If you're serious about recognizing your self-defeating attitudes and behaviors and then taking concrete steps to cultivate self-supporting attitudes and behaviors in your life, I want to leave you with one more thought:

As you're making these important life changes, please do *not* try to change other people along the way. This will only divert your energy from where it needs to be. (And guess what: you really can't change those other people, anyway!)

This project is between you and yourself.

WORKSHEET

MY PURPOSE, MY GOALS, MY SDABS AND SSABS

MY PURPOSE IN LIFE (In fifty words or less):

_____

_____

_____

_____

_____

_____

_____

_____

_____

_____

_____

WHAT WOULD SUCCESS LOOK LIKE FOR ME?

(Be as specific as possible):

_____

_____

_____

_____

_____

_____

_____

_____

_____

_____

_____

_____

MY GOALS
(Measurable, actionable goals that will show progress toward success):

_____
_____
_____
_____
_____
_____
_____
_____
_____
_____
_____
_____

Self-defeating attitudes and behaviors holding me back from reaching my goals:

1. _____
2. _____
3. _____

Three specific things I will STOP doing:

1. _____
2. _____
3. _____

Self-**supporting** attitudes and behaviors that I want to cultivate in my life:

1. _____
2. _____
3. _____

Three specific things I will START doing:

1. _____
2. _____
3. _____

CHAPTER 9:

CREATING YOUR IDEAL SELF

Walking into a room with confidence, looking everyone straight in the eye with a friendly smile, she catches the attention of the crowd with her captivating energy that makes for a bold presence before speaking any words . . .

She is able to connect with each and every person from different backgrounds and make them feel as if they are the most important person in the world. She picks up on social cues and personalities very quickly—she has a special instinct in which she is very sensitive to other people in the room.

She is independent and her confidence suggests that she refuses to let anyone else dictate the way she thinks about herself. Her work ethic is unquestioned.

She is genuine and a woman of her words. She understands that being seen as trustworthy comes down to holding true to her word. She is seen as a good and extremely loyal friend.

Although confident, she doesn't get mistaken for arrogant and she is known for being open-minded.

I do not see the girl described above as my "ideal" self of someone I simply hope to be, but I see it as my potential self—the person I will establish to become.

These words were written by a remarkable young woman named Michelle McMahon. The first time I met her, she was a freshman invited to walk onto the Michigan volleyball team.

And she was not happy.

In fact, as she would tell me later, it was the worst time of her life. A lifelong fan of Michigan sports, she had been thrilled and eager to come to the university and have the chance to wear the maize and blue.

She knew she would never play, because the coaches had told her so.

In a way, she was like many other athletes who had come into my office. She was a high achiever in high school, in both academics and athletics. She had come to the big university, and all of a sudden, she didn't stand out anymore. As she told me herself, she didn't even know who she was now.

So I started by telling her what I tell every athlete I see: I'm not going to guarantee you playing time. I'm not going to guarantee any kind of athletic success at all. All I will guarantee you is that when we're done here, you will know yourself better than you ever have before. And that will be your power.

"Volleyball is not who you are," I told her. (For more on this concept, see "Chapter 13: Your Sport Is What You Do, Not Who You Are.") I said, "Volleyball is just the stepping-stone that you're going to use to get to all the other places you will go in your life. And trust me, you're *going* to those places, because I can see that in you."

I could tell she was listening to me very carefully and that she wanted to believe what I was saying to her. But the problem was, she had no idea what her life would look like after volleyball. How could she get to a place that was so *great* if she had no idea what that place would even look like?

So I had her do an exercise that I've used many times in the past. I asked her to write out, in as much detail as she could, exactly the kind of person she wanted to become.

I didn't mean what kind of house she would live in or what kind of car she would drive, or even the job she would have ten years in the future. I wanted her to imagine what kind of person she wanted to become, what kind of values she would have, how other people would interact with her.

The next time I saw her, she had written the words that begin this chapter. And for all that I can see, in the years since graduating she has made every single word come true. She did finally play for the volleyball team as a senior, and when she moved to Chicago I stayed in touch with her. She called me one day and asked me if I thought she should hang on to a sales job she hated, or else pursue her dream to become a sports broadcaster.

I think you can probably guess the answer I gave her.

Right now, she's a studio host and sideline reporter on the Big Ten Network, and she also covers the Chicago Blackhawks for NBC Sports.

I didn't know exactly where she would end up, but as I told her that first day she walked into my office as a college freshman, I knew she'd be going someplace great.

In "Chapter 6: What Does Success Look Like?" I asked you to think about what success would look like for you if you were to sit down and try to describe it. That exercise fed into a few others: identifying the measurable, actionable goals that would demonstrate progress toward your version of success, then identifying the self-defeating attitudes and behaviors that might be holding you back from reaching those goals, and finally, determining the self-supporting attitudes and behaviors you could cultivate to put your life on the right track.

This exercise is just another way to look at where you want to be in your life. I encourage you to try it.

If there were absolutely no limits on your life, and you could become exactly the kind of person you wanted to be . . .

What would that look like?

Be as specific as you can. Write down every detail, because writing it all down is the first step to making it real.

Create this picture in your mind, just as if you were creating a scene in a movie, and write down everything you see, hear, taste, smell—everything.

I don't think you even realize how much power your mind has to shape who you are. Think about it. Everybody else is trying to influence you. Your television, advertisers, politicians, social media. The programming is happening all around you.

Why not program yourself?

But if you're still having trouble with this exercise—if you just can't manage to picture the ideal version of yourself—then I've got one more idea for you:

Instead of picturing yourself, picture the absolute best friend you could ever have. Everything about them—how reliable, how positive, how understanding, how compassionate, how strong, how wise, how *good* a person that friend would be.

What essential qualities and attributes should this person have to be your best friend, to be *the one person you could trust with your life*?

In my humble opinion, a best friend like that is someone who . . .

- believes in you,
- never wants to let you down,
- values your opinion,
- is happy when you do well,
- is honest with you.

What other qualities and attributes can you think of? Build that best friend you could ever have—every detail, from the ground up. The best friend to whom you would entrust your life.

(You already see where I'm going with this, don't you?)

That best friend is the person *you* want to become.

That very best friend, the one person you can trust with your life, should always be yourself.

YOUR VERY
BEST FRIEND
SHOULD ALWAYS
BE YOURSELF.

–GREG HARDEN

MICHELLE MCMAHON

TESTIMONIAL

Michelle McMahon was a walk-on volleyball player at the University of Michigan and is currently a studio host and sideline reporter for the Big Ten Network, as well as covering the Chicago Blackhawks for NBC Sports.

"Together, we're going to discover who you are."

The year I met Greg Harden, I was having the worst year of my life. I was a freshman walk-on to the volleyball team. I was at a point where I was about to mentally spiral, 1,000 percent depressed, although I didn't have the language for it and didn't really even understand what depression was at that point. I had so much anxiety, anxiety through the roof, to the point where I didn't want to go to practice so much, I'd actually make myself throw up in the bathroom. If you knew me then, you'd know that I really wasn't that person. My life had been pretty easy up until that point, but once I got to Michigan . . . well, being a walk-on, I already felt like a second-class citizen.

The whole experience of trying to be a Division I athlete was traumatic for me, but the silver lining was meeting Greg. If I hadn't met this man, I'm not sure I'd even be here right now. I was in a very scary place then. I was so closely identified with my sport, and it was such a huge part of my identity, if I had a bad practice or if I got yelled at, I would be destroyed.

When I walked into his office, day one, I didn't even know what I needed, but I knew I wasn't myself. I couldn't even put it into words. The only other people I could even talk to were my parents, and I didn't want to tell them just how bad it was for me, because I didn't want to scare them.

So I went to Greg's office, and the first hour, I just cried. Just water-works. Like a release of everything. When I was finally able to speak, I told him I didn't know what I was doing, didn't feel like I belonged at Michigan.

I was so lost, I didn't know who I was, didn't like the way I was acting, didn't know myself outside of volleyball, didn't know myself outside of being an athlete at Michigan. All of these foundations I thought I had built in my life were based on my past achievements.

But now those were all behind me. I was in a new place, starting over, and I had to rebuild myself from the ground up.

He told me, "I'm not going to guarantee you playing time. I'm not going to guarantee you success in volleyball. But what I will guarantee you is that you will know yourself better than any other person after I'm done working with you. And that is your power.

"And on top of that, the inner child in you needs to grow up."

I thought, *What?*

This was not the sympathetic voice I was expecting.

"Yeah, your situation sucks," he said, "and I don't discount that, but you can't control that, so let's focus on what you can control." That was my first indication that this wasn't going to be a bunch of hand-holding.

His advice was earth shattering for me. He told me, volleyball is not who you are. It's what you do, and you are going to use this as a stepping-stone to all of the other places you're going to go. And trust me, you are going to get to those places. Because I see that in you.

It's like he believed in me before *I* believed in me.

So I began the work. But how the hell was knowing myself going to help me with any of this? It sounded powerful, but I didn't understand the power in that moment. But I was ready to trust him and to start doing the work, because he was so confident in me as an individual and saw through any external circumstance that I was attaching to my identity. He had to wade through the mud with me, and he told me, we're going to get through this and we're going to get to who you really are as a person. We're going to discover together who you are.

The first thing he asked me: *Do you even know what it means to be assertive?*

I knew the word, but I didn't really know what it meant.

So he told me to go and work on it, to make it a project. To come back and explain to him what being assertive really means.

What I finally figured out was, if you're in a situation of conflict, or if you just need to address someone as an adult, you can't hold yourself responsible for their feelings. Regardless of how they handle the situation, you need to speak your truth. You need to do it in a respectful way, and then walk away knowing that you stood up for yourself.

I decided, I must practice, train, and rehearse being assertive through various opportunities life presents to me. The reactions of others are insignificant when I approach situations with assertiveness—the only thing that matters is how I feel afterward. If they do not value me as a person, at least they know that *I* value me as a person, human being, friend, girlfriend, sister, or teammate.

I put together a whole PowerPoint presentation for Greg, and this is one of the bullets I wrote: "Stop thinking about and caring what my friends, coaches, teammates, boyfriend or family members are thinking about me, and apply that focus to what I think of me and to what I aspire to be: to be sure of who I am, to know exactly what I stand for, and not be hesitant to stand up for myself."

I'm still learning these lessons as a young adult. I'm in a different world now, which is just as demanding, and you're constantly questioning yourself. Your identity and your own self-worth. You're being questioned by so many others.

It takes a lot of guts to be in this field I'm in. A lot of self-confidence, and I had none of that. If it wasn't for Greg, I wouldn't be in this position.

Everything that I learned in his office—I will have these moments in my life where I think I'm learning a new lesson, and then I stop and say, "Oh my God, Greg already taught me that."

CHAPTER 10:

ONLY AN ASSERTIVE YOU CAN BE A SUCCESSFUL YOU

I want to tell you about a young grad student named Emily Line. She had just completed her bachelor's degree at another school and had come to the University of Michigan to pursue a master's degree in social work. It's the same degree I started my career with, and a foundation for many people who go into counseling.

She called me at the office, told me she wanted to speak with me. Life gets busy, so it was another week before I finally got the chance to see her. It was the end of another hectic day.

"Thank you for meeting with me," this young woman said, shaking my hand. "I want to talk to you about the possibility of working with you as an intern."

I looked her in the eye. "I don't want an intern," I said. "I don't need an intern. I don't have *time* for an intern. So you have . . ."

I stopped, looked at my watch.

"Thirty minutes to convince me otherwise."

She just looked back at me, at a temporary loss for words.

I looked at my watch again. "Make that twenty-eight minutes."

So why did I talk to her this way? Seems kinda harsh, doesn't it? But here's the thing: Number one, I really didn't plan on having an intern that semester. And number two . . .

We'll call it a test. If she really was the right kind of person to work in my office, then this was a good way for her to prove it. If she didn't panic and fold under the pressure, maybe I could put her in front of a bunch of ego-driven high-performance individuals, not to mention their fire-breathing coaches.

We sat down in my office, she took a breath, and then she laid out her case. "This is the number one MSW program in the country," she said, "and I'm excited to be a part of it. But I've looked at all of the other internships that are available, and none of them are right for me."

She went on to tell me about her life. On the surface, I could already have made some prejudgments about her: white, blond, just graduated from one of the most expensive private colleges in the state. A privileged, sheltered life, I might have assumed. But there was so much more to her story. She was only a middle school student when her sister was diagnosed with leukemia. Emily was the right match and became a bone marrow donor. She did it without a second thought.

Sadly, her sister would not survive the disease, but the experience changed Emily. "Even in my sister's short life," she told me, "I can never remember a moment, even when she was in great pain, where she didn't find a way to be happy."

I kept listening.

"That's why I never want to be put into a box," she said. "Here at this school, or wherever I end up working. Because what if tomorrow is my last day? I just want the opportunity to have a life where every day I feel like I have a purpose and a chance to be happy."

"The internship programs we have here at the university," I said, "they're just guides. You don't have to let them chart your territory."

"I know," she said. "That's why I'm here."

I remember the next moment vividly. I dropped my head, rubbed one hand through my hair. She was too good, had too much hunger for this, for me to pass up. She projected confidence and was passionate about helping and serving others.

"I'm going to have to see you on Monday," I said. "Nine o'clock. Don't be late."

In the previous four chapters, we've been talking about defining what success looks like to you, setting real goals, and then identifying the attitudes and behaviors that either defeat or support your efforts to achieve those goals. I even took a slightly different approach and asked you to describe, in vivid detail, the *ideal you*. Take it all together, and it boils down to me trying to get you to see what works in your life and what doesn't, and then to take *tangible, identifiable, measurable* steps to deliberately and intentionally reprogram and reengineer your own life.

But here's something important: It's not enough just to have a list of positive steps that will make your life better. You also have to make sure that you're always giving yourself the best possible chance to take those steps successfully. And to do that, you must learn to become more assertive.

Now, what does that even mean?

Admit it, as soon as you heard the word "assertive," you may have immediately pictured a certain type of person. You're picturing the guy who cuts you off in traffic, who shouts down anybody who dares to disagree with him, who takes the last slice of pizza without a second thought for anyone else. (I'm saying "guy" here, but of course there's a female version, too.) But what you're picturing is someone I'd call *aggressive, thoughtless*, a *bully*. And maybe a few other words that are even stronger.

That person is not who I'm talking about! And I'd never ask you to be that person.

I'm asking you to think about being *assertive* as an essential part of achieving your goals, but being assertive in the best, most positive way.

So what does that mean?

According to the dictionary, "assertive" means "disposed to or characterized by bold or confident statements and behavior." But for me, the way I'm talking about it here, being assertive means being able to have your needs met while still interacting with great sensitivity to those around you.

- It means *valuing yourself*—valuing your own life, your own goals, your own precious time here on this earth—while at the same time valuing others.
- It means recognizing that you have a God-given right to pursue

happiness and every other good and worthy thing in life. And that you don't have to put anyone else down to lift yourself up.

- It means standing up for what you believe in and expressing your own feelings and opinions in a direct and appropriate way.
- It means taking responsibility for your actions, recognizing your achievements, owning your mistakes.
- It means knowing that for you to *win* doesn't have to mean that someone else must *lose*.
- It means always being honest, within respectful bounds. (As the Dalai Lama said, "If you are honest, truthful, and transparent, people trust you. If people trust you, you have no grounds for fear, suspicion, or jealousy.")
- It means protecting yourself and not allowing others to violate your rights or infringe on your happiness or peace of mind.
- It means being less concerned about what others think of you and more concerned with who you aspire to *be*.

Being assertive is all about giving yourself the four A's that we identified in "Chapter 8: The Angel on Your Right Shoulder: Self-Supporting Attitudes and Behaviors." *Self-attention, self-affection, self-approval,* and *self-acceptance.*

In other words, *self-love.*

We've all known people who constantly put themselves first and never think of anyone else. I *know* you're not that kind of person, or you would never have gotten this far into this book.

We've also known people who constantly put other people's needs ahead of their own. Sounds more like you, at least most of the time? If so, let me just ask you:

How's that working out for you?

Just take a moment and think about what being assertive—in this best, positive, respectful, life-affirming, self-loving way—could do for you. And why you *need* to find a way to make this a part of your life. All the other changes we're talking about in this book are not going to happen until you *decide* you deserve to make them happen—even if that means respectfully letting other people know that your own needs are *at least* as important as theirs.

I've seen this quick, useful guide attributed to a number of different sources. We'll call it the *three C's of assertive communication*:

1. Confidence. You believe in yourself, your message, and your ability to handle the situation.
2. Clarity. Your message is clear and easy to understand.
3. Control. You deliver your message in a calm and controlled manner, tracking the other person's reaction.

I know that communicating assertively can be tough for many people (especially, but not exclusively, for many women). But you *need* to be assertive. You need to be not just your own best friend but also your own best *advocate* if you're going to be successful.

EMILY LINE

TESTIMONIAL

Emily Line is one of the few interns who worked directly with Greg. She has an amazing story of how she persuaded him to give her this opportunity, then used the insights she gained in that time throughout the rest of her life. As Greg says, "Emily's assertive communication techniques were so well developed that her career became unlimited. She started as a clinical therapist and licensed social worker, then became a top salesperson, and is now the technology VP at the National Association of Realtors, the largest trade association in the country."

**"Dream hard, execute big, and above all,
make sure your heart speaks to your mind."**

I was thinking about what kind of internship I wanted to do when I was at Michigan, getting my Master of Social Work degree. I went through the book of available internships, and I didn't see anything that felt right to me—but I had heard of this "living legend" named Greg Harden.

I knew he had an MSW degree, too, and I decided, yep, this is the guy I want to learn from.

It was the most difficult interview I've ever had in my life.

I contacted him and I asked to have a talk with him, told him I was pursuing the same degree he had and I wanted to share some thoughts on how I might be able to help him as an intern. He said, "Sure, I can talk to you next week."

So I go the athletic department and I'm ready to talk to him. He shakes my hand firmly, looks me in the eye, and says, "I don't want an intern, I don't need an intern, I don't have time for an intern. So you have . . ."

He stops and looks at his watch.

"Exactly thirty minutes," he continues. "Actually, now you have twenty-eight minutes to convince me otherwise."

What I actually said to him is kind of a blur to me now. I had no idea how that was going to go. I'm a relationship-based person, and even now when I'm in the tech field, I still believe in the power of relationships.

I looked at him and I said, you know that the U-M MSW program is the number one program in America, and I'm so excited to be a part of it. But when I started looking at the different opportunities within the program, I felt frustrated because it felt like I was going to be put into a box. I was struggling with that, because even though I'm not driven by money, I still want to be independent and to have a lifestyle within this profession where I can be happy. Social work may get all the warm fuzzies, but it's one of those fields where you just frankly don't ever make any money.

I had just graduated from a private college, which was pretty expensive at the time, and now I'm entering grad school at U-M, and at the end of it, I want to be able to do something good that has an impact on other people, but at the same time I don't want to be saddled with a lot of debt and eating ramen noodles.

We talked it through, and Greg said, "We're going to give you a road map that's going to change your mind on trying to fit into the path that you see in front of you. Those paths you think you're limited to are good guides, but they won't chart your course. I can see that you have a hunger to have more than what's being laid out in front of you. Ultimately, the degree you get here will not determine your worth—your worth will be determined by what you deliver."

I told Greg how inspired I had already been, reading some of the stories about his counseling. As a middle school child, I was a bone marrow donor to my sister, who would later die from leukemia. That has always been a motivator for me, finding ways to overcome the limitations that life puts on us. Even in my sister's short life, I can never remember a moment, even when she was in great pain, when she didn't find a way to be happy.

I don't want to get put into a box, because what if tomorrow is my last day? I want the opportunity to have a life where every day I feel like I have a purpose and a chance to be happy.

After I graduated from U-M with my MSW, I was dying to move to Chicago. Greg told me, be passionate about this personally, and the professional will follow. If the opportunity you see is in business development (a fancy term for sales), then you can be a counselor in sales. Just go and be where you want to be.

That's how I ended up working first for a racetrack, then an insurance company, and then I was recruited by the National Association of Realtors, where I've been ever since.

I'm in a very demanding technical field now, but all of the lessons that Greg taught me are still with me, and so often I'll find myself pausing and remembering Greg's ideas. The time I spent with him has had such a huge impact on all of the communicating I do now, whether it's with my team or with members of other organizations we're working with. Just the other day, I texted him and said, "How is it that you never leave my head?"

There was a major deal that we were trying to put together, and it was crashing. All of a sudden, I looked across the table and I realized that we had been leading with our objectives and I hadn't listened enough to understand what a true partnership should look like. So I started asking questions and listening more, because this was a very large national partnership that would have a big effect on the industry. I could see it in the expressions on the other people's faces and I said to myself, we're being so selfish right now. We need to figure out what their endgame is and make sure we create a mutually beneficial partnership. If I get what I want for our organization but they don't get what they want for theirs, the whole deal is going to fail as soon as we start.

Here is one of the best things Greg ever taught me—something I say to myself over and over:

Dream hard, execute big, and above all, make sure your heart speaks to your mind.

From the very first time I met him, Greg saw a lifelong fear of failing in my eyes. An obsession with perfection. "There's no such thing as perfect," he told me. "There's just finding the right way for *you*." He helped me to reframe my fears and to think of them as opportunities instead. There have been many moments in my life where I've tried to avoid risk, to play it safe, and quite frankly that's just the wrong approach. He has always reminded me that you can't truly fail if you have a clear idea of what the opportunities look like and you have plans for making the most of them.

Greg created not a black-and-white piece of art for me, but one with a lot of colors.

CHAPTER 11

THE 100 PERCENT CHALLENGE

When I got my bachelor's degree but before I had done any graduate work, I was eager to find a career. I was known as a "health nut" back then, so I thought what the hell, I'm going to start my own health club, with a nice health food restaurant attached to it. To get to that goal, I figured I'd start out in the health field and quickly work my way up to management.

I targeted several companies in the health industry. Every single one of them turned me down. Finally, I took a gamble and walked into a Vic Tanny International. If you're of a certain age, you might recognize that name. Vic Tanny had over a hundred clubs all over the country. He was one of the first owners to turn sweaty muscle-head "gyms" into modern, well-appointed "health clubs."

I'll never forget that day. Sam and Bob were the managers, and they both had to hide their amusement when I walked in off the street and suggested that I should be on their management team. After they made it crystal clear that this fantasy wasn't going to come true, I went to plan B:

"So hire me as a fitness instructor," I said. I was in superior shape then, with 4 percent body fat. What more could they want?

"We don't need any more instructors," they said. "But we do need a porter."

They were surprised when I immediately said, "I'm your man."

Now, I know what you're thinking. Isn't "porter" just a fancy word for "janitor?"

Yes! But unlike most people who would find themselves in such a job, I decided that I would have no problem with whatever task they assigned me. It was a conscious choice. I cleaned the carpets; I emptied the trash cans; I cleaned the sweat off the mirrors and scum off the showers. I sanitized the toilets and the urinals.

And most importantly, I gave 100 percent, 100 percent of the time.

I engaged with everybody I met in that club. I treated each person as if they were the most valued employee or customer in the world. I "whistled while I worked," and I tried to lift the spirits of everyone else in that environment. And yes, not only did I still clean and polish the urinals, I did it as if I were cleaning and polishing my Rolls-Royce.

As Martin Luther King, Jr. said, "If a man is called to be a street sweeper, he should sweep streets even as Michelangelo painted, or Beethoven composed music."

I was just a porter, but I never forgot: *That job was not who I was; it was simply what I was given to do.*

I made the deliberate and intentional *decision* to be the absolute best at doing this job. No one would ever be a better porter, period. And no one would study the day-to-day operations of a health club better than I, from my unique vantage point of seeing it from the ground up.

Within six months, I was the club's assistant manager.

Your commitment to consistently perform at the highest level possible, to project a positive attitude, will support your quest to climb to the top of any industry.

It's one of the most productive habits you can ever develop—one of the most important things that I'm going to say to you in this book:

Practice, train, and rehearse giving 100 percent, 100 percent of the time.

I see young athletes in my office every day, and for many of them, their first year in college is a *huge* adjustment. Think about it. They were given certain physical gifts that made them *stars* in high school. Most never had to work hard or give 100 percent to succeed, to be the center of attention, to have articles written about them in the local paper. Many of them never had to work hard in the classroom, either, because frankly, academics was rarely the top priority.

So now here they are at the University of Michigan, surrounded—for the first time in their lives—by athletes who are just as good as they are. The social and academic pressures are suddenly beyond anything they've ever experienced before. And even in their sport, the one place where they excelled, they are forced to actually work hard in practice and to develop their bodies, instead of just relying on their God-given talents.

That's often when I encounter these young men and women: just as they're dealing with all these challenges. One of the most important things I always try to do is turn these challenges into something *fun*.

That's right: FUN!

Imagine I'm talking to a young man from the inner city or from a small town in the middle of Indiana, a kid who's never excelled at anything except basketball. Turn this into a *game*, I tell him. A competition with yourself. Just try it out for one semester. In your schoolwork, give 100 percent, 100 percent of the time. How *fun* would it be to make the dean's list? How *fun* would it be to shatter everyone's expectations for you? To destroy the stereotype that people have in their minds because of how you look and where you came from? You came here to shoot a basketball through a hoop and you're on the *dean's list*? You can whip everyone's ass both on the court and in the classroom? Can you even imagine how much *fun* it would be to blow everyone's mind like that?

Of course, in doing that, you'll be training yourself to be self-motivated, to be self-disciplined. You're going to be training yourself to have the mind of a champion, which is going to make you a better person. Which is going to make you *an even better athlete*.

You're training yourself not to be lazy. To rise to *any* challenge. You're proving to yourself that *anything* you put your mind to, whatever you commit to, you can achieve.

And remember, we're talking about the stuff that you don't even *like*! You're training yourself to give 100 percent, 100 percent of the time, at the stuff that doesn't appeal to you, that doesn't come naturally to you.

The greatest competition you're ever going to face is yourself. If you can take yourself on and be better than you were yesterday, you can take on anybody. So imagine this for me:

If you train yourself to give 100 percent, 100 percent of the time, to the stuff you *hate*, how phenomenal are you going to be when you get to the stuff you *love*?

This is where I'm trying to take you, and as I said earlier, it's one of the most important things I'm going to say to you in this entire book:

If you make it your mindset, your vision of who you are, that you're going to make it a *habit* to give 100 percent, 100 percent of the time, in everything you do—if you make that your norm, your base level, your default mode—then on your absolutely worst day, even when you slip, *you're still going to be better than the average person on their* BEST *day.*

PRACTICE
TRAIN &
REHEARSE
GIVING 100%
100% **OF THE TIME.**

—GREG HARDEN

CHAPTER 12

ADAPT OR DIE!

This may be the harshest title in the whole book, but hear me out.

I had the privilege of working with a young man, Michael Powers, who had severe anger issues. It was so bad, I wasn't just worried about him, I was worried about anyone else in the world who might happen to make him angry, intentionally or unintentionally. And if there was ever a person who deserved to be pissed off at the world, Michael, with his long history of abuse, betrayal, and a life-threatening illness, was that guy.

I worked with him for months, and then finally, out of desperation, I encouraged him to study a martial art—something that could help him tame his anger and channel it into a new form of physical and mental discipline. Great idea, right?

When he came to me and told me that he signed up for his first class, I was ecstatic. "What's the style?" I said. "Tai chi? Aikido?" Either of those arts seemed a great fit for him.

"Ninjutsu," he said.

I tried not to look horrified. Ninjutsu was the ancient art practiced by the spies and professional assassins of feudal Japan, known as the ninjas. Had I really just incited this young man with all the anger issues to learn the lethal skills of a ninja?

I decided to hold my tongue for the time being, but I monitored the situation carefully. As the classes progressed, I began to see an improvement in the way this young man carried himself. But it wasn't until I met his sensei and his fellow students that I was totally convinced he had made the right decision to study this art. Far from turning him into an assassin, it was instead helping him become more flexible, more mindful, more at peace with himself and everyone else around him. His self-awareness and mental discipline had started to become his strengths.

When I was invited to give the students a "mental fitness" seminar, I jumped at the chance to finally observe the class in person and to meet Sensei Rob Byas. I could sense almost immediately that Rob was not only an exceptional martial artist but also a brilliant man—he could see each student's strengths and weaknesses and then challenge that person to see him- or herself more clearly.

I watched some of the training and appreciated how, with Sensei Byas, the emphasis was on *defense*, not on attacking. These students were being trained to use their bodies in the modes of the four elements—earth, water, fire, and wind—and to develop the ability to defend and protect themselves and those around them, turning any available item or opportunity into a weapon.

When I was done presenting my mental-fitness seminar, the sensei gave me a T-shirt with "ADAPT or DIE!" in bold block letters across the chest. That's when it hit me: this was the central theme of the class, of the sensei's lessons, of the art of ninjutsu itself:

ADAPT OR DIE. You train yourself to adapt to every possible circumstance, deal with any situation, use any object as a weapon to defend yourself.

You adjust your thinking based on the changes that confront you. You roll with the punches. You improvise. You *adapt*.

Or else you *die*.

In purely biological terms, it really is that stark. Charles Darwin's immortal body of work boiled down to those three words: ADAPT OR DIE. When the physical conditions around you change, either you adapt to them, or you perish forever (and all your potential future descendants will never exist). You're here today, reading this book, precisely because you come from a long line of ancestors who found a way to adapt when they had to.

But even if you take away the literal life-and-death stakes, the phrase still has a profound meaning. Take a moment and think about all the successful people you've met in your life. The top-flight athletes, the influential leaders, the peak performers in every avenue of life. Out of all the qualities that these people have in common, how important is *adaptability*?

We all have to deal with change. Big or small, positive or negative, change is all around us, every day. Sometimes, you can see it coming. Just as often, you can't. How do *you* respond to change? Does it overwhelm you? Stress you out? Paralyze you?

Take a moment and write down all the words and phrases that come to mind when you think about the word "change." I did this with a group once, and here are some of the more negative responses:

- *Change brings anxiety.*
- *Change means discomfort.*
- *The prospect of change fills me with dread.*
- *Fear of the unknown stops me every time.*
- *Why change now?*
- *It will take me out of my comfort zone.*
- *I'm too old to start over.*

Do any of these look familiar? How many would you write down if I challenged you to do the same? Be honest!

I challenged the group to make a new list, imagining only those traits that would lead to success. Here were some of the answers:

- *I need a boost of enthusiasm in my life.*
- *I know that embracing optimism will open new doors.*
- *I know this will take courage, but I'm ready.*
- *If I don't have passion for what I'm doing, I've already failed.*
- *Just show me an opportunity; I can take it from there.*

- *Good things come from adapting to a challenge.*
- *I want to take myself to a place I've never been before.*
- *I want to become a better person.*
- *It's time for something new.*

Imagine the power of thinking this way. Imagine the power of not just accepting change, but managing change, *embracing* change.

Of choosing to be a *victor*, not a *victim*.

The only thing that will *never* change in your life is the simple fact that *change will always be part of your life.*

So how are you going to deal with it?

CHANGE IS THE INEVITABLE,
THAT WHICH CANNOT BE
AVOIDED OR EVADED.
YOU CAN BE A
PART OF CHANGE
OR YOU CAN HAVE
YOUR ASS KICKED.
YOU DECIDE.

—GREG HARDEN

CHAPTER 13

YOUR SPORT IS WHAT YOU DO,
NOT WHO YOU ARE

I'm going to start this story with another troubled young athlete sitting in my office chair, but this time there's a twist.

The athlete's name was Samantha Arsenault. This was the year 2000, just a few months after the Summer Olympics in Sydney. Samantha swam the leadoff leg in the 4x200-meter freestyle relay, then watched as her childhood hero, Jenny Thompson, brought the team home on the anchor leg.

First place. Olympic record. A gold medal for young Samantha.

She was eighteen years old, already an Olympic gold medalist, and now a freshman at the University of Michigan, ready to begin her college career.

Stop and think about that for a moment. Out of all the first-year athletes who have sat in my office, ready to start their careers at Michigan, how many of them do you think had already reached the highest possible level of achievement in their sport? (I'm not counting Michael Phelps here, because he came to Michigan to train with his coach, and he happened to do some volunteer assistant coaching while he was here.)

Samantha Arsenault was one of the few student athletes who ever came to Michigan as a freshman with an Olympic medal already around her neck.

And she was a pretty unhappy eighteen-year-old.

For one thing, she had been nursing a serious shoulder injury that she suffered in training for the Olympics. She swam through the pain in Sydney and didn't want to interrupt her career now with surgery and a long recovery. She had come to Michigan with unbelievably high expectations, both internally and externally, and she was terrified at the thought of letting anyone down. She had to keep swimming.

It was all Samantha knew how to do. Since she was a child, she would get up at 5:00 a.m. almost every day so one of her parents could take her to swim practice. For literally as long as she could remember, her entire sense of self-worth had been based entirely on her performance as a swimmer.

And now, for the first time in her life, with her own body threatening to fail her, she was facing at least the *possibility* of a life out of the water.

It was terrifying.

"Samantha," I said, "if you see yourself only as a swimmer, you're doomed."

I still remember the numb look on her face when she heard that.

"I get it," I said. "You've been swimming your whole life. It's all you've ever known. And you must *love* it, or you wouldn't have gotten to where you are. But when a sport is all you know, it can become *who you are*. 'This is why other people love me! This is why they cheer for me!' All these amazing things that swimming has done for you—how could you *not* see yourself as a swimmer, right?"

She nodded her head.

"I don't blame you for seeing yourself this way," I said. "I really don't. It makes total sense! And it makes total sense that you're terrified right now. But what are you going to do next?"

She didn't have an answer for that. I think that's how I already knew she was such a remarkable person. She didn't have the answer, and she was smart enough to come to me, to see if I could help her find it.

"You have a choice right now," I said. "You can wallow in your fear and self-doubt, the two greatest enemies you'll ever face on this earth, or we can work together to help you start redefining yourself. To redesign, reshape, reconstruct how you see yourself and how you see your world."

As I do with so many people, I went right to the punch line: CONTROL THE CONTROLLABLES.

"In your current circumstances," I said, "what can you control? Can you control the fact that you're injured, other than just doing your physical therapy?"

"No."

"Can you control other people's expectations?"

"No."

"How they see you? What they think of you?"

"No."

"That's right," I said. "In fact, the only thing you even have a *shot* at controlling is *how you see yourself.* How you respond to this adversity. How you reframe your own thoughts. Because thoughts are *real*, Samantha. And the thoughts you've been having, how scared you are—it's all to be expected if you're a human being. If you're a robot, then you get a pass. Nothing to worry about, go to the shop and get your shoulder repaired. You're good to go. But if you're a real human being, then what does that mean? It means you're getting tested right now. And you have the opportunity, right now, to *decide* what kind of person you're going to be."

Everything I was telling her was building up to this major theme and critical thinking point:

"You've got to decide that *with or without your sport*, your life is going to be amazing."

The way Samantha's life had gone, she had to learn this lesson quickly. It was a real crash course for her. But she was so driven, so determined to be good at whatever she tried, that I wasn't surprised to see all the amazing things she's done since that day.

After a year at Michigan, she transferred to Georgia, where she did get the chance to achieve some more great things in the pool as she helped carry the Bulldogs swim team to a national championship in her senior year—this after having to miss a year when doctors found a tumor inside her body.

Since retiring from the sport, Samantha has become an amazing motivational speaker and entrepreneur. She is also an amazing mother, who had to live through a parent's ultimate nightmare when one of her four daughters spent forty-one days in the hospital with a serious heart condition, fighting for her life. That daughter is doing great now, and for eighteen years, Samantha Arsenault—now Samantha Livingstone—has been traveling the country giving speeches and leading seminars, working with athletes of all ages and women in business organizations. I encourage you to seek out her TEDx talk called "The Weight of Gold: An Olympian's Path to Recovery."

She's having an amazing life, just as I knew she would—with or without swimming.

So whether you're a high-performance athlete or striving to be an exceptional business professional, I understand how and why you love the attention and approval of fans, family, friends, peers, and bosses when you're victorious. If you're a swimmer, I can't blame you if you *live* for that moment when your country's flag is raised while the national anthem is played and you stand on the podium with a gold medal around your neck.

But when you really think about it, no matter what it is that you do, I hope you start to realize that there *has* to be more to you than just this one dimension. Your sense of self-worth, your self-esteem—it *can't* be based solely on these external forces in your life.

Because what happens if those things go away? Being a hero, being popular, thousands of people screaming your name—do you think that can last forever? For *anyone*?

Your body grows old. Your beauty fades. And all the things you may *think* you need to be happy—fame, money, power, influence—they are all so fleeting. (And how happy can those things really make you, anyway? You think there aren't unhappy and depressed multimillionaires who wish for more in life than just their wealth?)

Ultimately, you can't let your self-worth be determined by the trappings of this world, because those will ultimately fail you.

You have to learn to construct in yourself a person who is invested in self-love and self-acceptance. You can decide—win, lose, or draw—that you're going to enjoy your life and love yourself, flaws and all.

You can decide, just as Samantha did, that *with or without* . . .

- your sport,
- your job,
- your title,

and no matter . . .

- the size of your house,
- the kind of car you drive,
- how many people know your name,
- how many people like/follow/friend you on Twitter/Facebook/Instagram/whatever,
- or what people say about you on Twitter/Facebook/Instagram/whatever,

. . . you are going to have an amazing life!

IF BEATING YOURSELF UP EVERY DAY
WORKS FOR YOU, HAVE AT IT!
IF YOU'RE HAPPY BEING MISERABLE,
THEN BY ALL MEANS CONTINUE!
BUT IF THOSE THINGS ARE
NOT WORKING FOR YOU... YOU
NEED TO RECALIBRATE, REFRAME,
DEPROGRAM, AND REPROGRAM
HOW YOU SEE YOURSELF AND HOW
YOU TALK TO YOURSELF.

—GREG HARDEN

MICHAEL PARKE

TESTIMONIAL

Michael Parke played soccer at Michigan and is currently a professor of organizational behavior at the London Business School.

**"Enter a boy with blinders.
Exit a young man without them."**

I was a soccer player at Michigan and came into my sophomore year fully believing that I'd be a starter. But of course, life doesn't always pan out the way we plan. I was injured during the preseason practices, and when I came back I thought I was playing very well, but I ended up beginning the season as the reserve left back, with little chance for playing time.

I felt that my life was defined by soccer, but because I wasn't playing, I fell into a fog of depression for a good month and a half.

That's when I went to see G.

As soon as I started talking, it was all about how unfair it was, that my coaches were treating some players differently, that I never got the chance to prove myself because of my injury, that I could be one of the best players on the team if the coaches just believed in me. And on and on.

G stopped me, right in the middle of my whining and complaining. "Life is not fair, son. What are you going to do about it?"

I spent the next few minutes just listening to him.

"This is not about soccer. This is about you becoming a man. Your job is to be as confident as you can be, regardless of what the coaches think of you. And to be ready, so that when your opportunity comes, you can take hold of it and never look back.

"Stop trying to change your coaches. Focus on what you can control.

CONTROL THE CONTROLLABLES. Practice, train, and rehearse giving 100 percent until your coaches have no choice but to play you.

"You are so much more than just a soccer player. Soccer is something you do. Just like school, just like relationships. If you're not happy, change it. And avoid that depressing clan you hang around with on the bench."

I knew what he was talking about. There was a whole group of reserves who would get into a little huddle, talking about the coaches, about the other players.

"Their depression wears on you," G said. "They don't mean any harm, but they're making it so hard for you to be happy and confident."

The message was so simple, but it was a real slap in the face. The blinders were off. I could see exactly what I needed to do.

I'm not saying I never had any setbacks again. It took time and hard work to build this new outlook on life and to start this journey that would lead me to where I am today.

I did end up playing that year. By the time I was a senior, I was a starter and captain of the team. Today, I'm a professor of organizational behavior at the London Business School, and I still apply many of the lessons that G taught me at Michigan.

Greg Harden painted a picture of life I'd never seen before, a reality I'd never dreamed of or thought possible. But with his guidance, I started to dream. I started to believe, and I made giant strides toward becoming the person I wanted to be.

I hope his words help give you the same opportunity to embark on your own journey.

CHAPTER 14

WHAT DO YOU DO WHEN
YOU LOSE EVERYTHING?

As long as I'm talking to you about making your life amazing with or without your sport, your job, your title, your *anything*, let me tell you a story about a young football player who had the whole world by the tail:

His name is Warde Manuel. He played football at Brother Martin High School in New Orleans. When he graduated in 1986, he didn't just become a First-Team High School All-American, he was named the defensive captain. This is back in the day when the All-America team was flown out to California to visit Hollywood. Not a bad start on life for an eighteen-year-old in a sports culture that treated high school stars like celebrities.

He received a scholarship to the University of Michigan. That's how I came to know him. He was a defensive lineman, and all linemen at Michigan follow a predictable trajectory: you redshirt as a freshman. You work out, gain muscle mass, build a body that's suitable for college ball. As a "redshirt freshman" (academically, a sophomore), if you're good enough, you start to see limited time on the field as a backup. Because of that redshirt, you've got three more years of eligibility left. By this time, you've matured into your body, you've seen a little time on the field, so now, when you're a junior or a senior, you'll finally get a chance to fight for a starting spot.

Warde Manuel *started* as a redshirt freshman, at multiple positions.

He was versatile enough and quick enough to start as both a defensive lineman and an outside linebacker. He received the Frederick Matthaei Award as the top junior-to-be coming into the 1988 season. He had every physical and mental tool to become a college star, and his path to the NFL was all but guaranteed—because modern NFL teams absolutely *salivate* over big, quick, smart defensive linemen.

But then it all went off the rails.

Warde got hurt. A serious neck injury. He tried to play through it, but his own body soon made it clear to him: your football career is over.

From a very early age, Warde Manuel had defined himself as a football player and nothing else. The game had made him a star. It had kept his name in the newspapers and in the college scouting reports. It had brought him from defensive captain of the High School All-America team all the way to Michigan to play for Bo Schembechler. By all rights, the game should have taken him to the NFL draft and a payday of many millions of dollars.

But now the journey was over.

I watched Warde endure his own crisis of identity. He suffered depression and despair. But he stayed at Michigan to finish his undergraduate degree, and now he had to make a choice for the rest of his life. He had to reinvent, rediscover, redefine himself. He had to *deprogram* and *reprogram* his own self-definition.

There were other people in his life, even advisers at the university, telling him that he should go learn a trade so he could find a good job as soon as possible. Against all this advice, Warde stayed at Michigan and went to grad school. He earned a master's in social work. And then he earned a master's in business administration.

As it turned out, he wasn't just good at tackling running backs and rushing the quarterback. He was a brilliant young man in many other ways—not just academically, but in his solid common sense, in his ability to see the world and to read people. He had all these amazing attributes that we may never have seen if he hadn't gotten hurt. But now, with an MSW and an MBA, he became a businessman with the perceptions of a social scientist.

He left Michigan to join the athletic administration at Georgia Tech. Came back to Michigan and became an assistant athletic director, then an associate athletic director, all while grinding on his MBA. He left Michigan again, became the athletic director at the University at Buffalo. He transformed one of the most moribund cultures in all Division I, increasing the school's athletics budget from $11 million to $25 million within three years.

He left to become the athletic director at the University of Connecticut, where he helped the school achieve the unprecedented double feat of national championships in women's basketball *and* men's basketball.

Warde was more than an athlete. His life had become amazing, and he never looked back or felt sorry for himself.

And then he came back to become the athletic director at Michigan. My old protégé became my boss and convinced me not to retire. Imagine that!

Not too bad for a kid who was never going to be anything but a football player.

There is only one species on this earth whose members can transform themselves and alter how they see themselves and their world. As changes come into your life, as a member of the human race, you can decide to be happy or sad, positive or negative, committed or disconnected. You can decide how you're going to react to those changes, whether they are as gradual as aging or as sudden as a career-ending injury to a young athlete.

I'm going to repeat the same sentence I said in "Chapter 12: Adapt or Die!" because it may be the one biggest challenge you will ever face: The only thing that *won't* change is the simple fact that *change will always be part of your life.*

If the change is as dramatic as the end of your life's dream, as it was for Warde Manuel, it takes a special kind of person, with a special kind of attitude, to find a new dream.

Ask yourself honestly: *Would I be able to do that?*

WARDE MANUEL

TESTIMONIAL

A first-team high school All-American in Louisiana, Warde Manuel came to Michigan to play football for Bo Schembechler. His dream of playing in the NFL was dashed in 1989 when he suffered a career-ending neck injury. After receiving master's degrees in both social work and business administration and working in the Michigan Athletic Department, he left to become the athletic director at the University at Buffalo, then at the University of Connecticut. In 2016, he returned to the University of Michigan as the school's thirteenth athletic director.

"Don't celebrate negativity."

It's so important for our young student athletes to understand that at some point it could all be taken away from you. It wasn't that I decided to give up football. The injury was such that I *could not* play football anymore.

Greg was there to help me see that my life was going to be amazing, even without a career in the NFL. His message has always been about not making any excuses about where you are in your life or how you got there. What you do is prepare yourself and continue to work on yourself and who you are, so that you can drive your own and others' success in life. He has prepared me to have success wherever I've gone.

Greg says, "Let's not have a pity party," because it does no good to wallow in the negative. If you're thinking about it all the time, like "Woe is me," it's like you're *celebrating* negativity by letting it occupy your mind all the time.

Greg's message has always been: *Let's recognize our mistakes; let's put ourselves on the road to making the changes that are necessary so those mistakes don't happen again. What do you learn from them?*

Let's move on, so we're stronger than we were before.

It's not like, when something bad happens in your life, you're supposed to stop thinking about it. It's going to bother you; it's going to put you back on your heels a little bit. The message is, don't let it be the *only* thing that you think about.

Don't let it stop you from finding a new way forward.

A few more words from Greg on Warde Manuel:

Hold up! Wait a minute.

I would be remiss if I did not share with you just how much Warde J. Manuel changed *my* life and *my* career and how he forced me to evolve and create a whole new approach in helping and serving others.

I had come to athletics as a clinical therapist and alcohol/drug specialist, while Warde came from New Orleans, and let's just say that he loved to have a good ol' time. Hence, he was directed to spend some time with me, and I helped him start to examine his lifestyle and decision-making.

After several meetings, Warde made it clear to me that he did not need a "shrink." He just needed someone to trust and confide in, someone to give him real-world advice. He told me that if I wasn't going to treat him like I cared about him as a real person and not as a "patient," then he wasn't interested in coming in to see me.

Imagine a college kid telling me that! But what he said was exactly what I needed to hear.

Warde set in motion a dynamic that pushed me to change and adapt, to determine and quickly assess who needed clinical intervention and who simply needed an adult ally and advocate. I will always be grateful for that opportunity to become a better counselor and a better person.

Thanks, Warde!

CHAPTER 15

A MATTER OF TRUST

"Coach Schembechler wants you to come talk to his players."

The call came in 1986 when I was still working at the hospital in Ypsilanti. The man on the other end of the line was a member of the football team's staff. He told me that Coach Schembechler wanted me to come in and do a lecture for his players on the dangers of drug and alcohol abuse.

I thought about it for about three seconds and said, "No, thank you."

There was a long pause on the line. I was pretty sure this was not the answer he was expecting. This was Michigan football, after all. And this request was coming straight from the legend himself.

The staff member finally spoke: "May I ask why you're declining?"

"Because what you're asking me to do is to come in and give them a forty-minute rah-rah talk on why drugs and alcohol are bad for you, think about your future, you gotta make good decisions, 'Just say no,' thank you very much, goodbye. And that's not going to do *anything* for *anybody*. So I'd rather just pass and not waste everyone's time."

The staff member thanked me and hung up. I never thought I'd hear from him again. But two weeks later, he called again. This time, he said, "Coach Schembechler wants to meet you."

"Who else is going to be there?" I said.

"Excuse me?"

"I'd like the athletic director to be in this meeting. Along with the head trainer, and everyone else who'd need to be involved with a drug-and-alcohol treatment program."

He probably thought I was nuts—I *was* nuts—but he agreed to invite everyone to what would quite possibly be my public execution.

The day of the meeting came. I went down to the athletic department. Now, everybody who knows anything about college football knows who Bo Schembechler was. He took over as coach in 1969, at a time when the football program had been struggling for years, and by the end of summer two-a-days, 65 out of his 140 players had quit the team. "Those who stay will be champions," he famously said, and the team closed out the season by beating Ohio State, led by his old friend and boss Woody Hayes, in a game that is still considered one of the greatest upsets of all time. In twenty-one seasons as head coach, his teams would win 194 games and thirteen Big Ten Championships.

But those are just the numbers. What they don't capture is the character of the man himself, and just how captivating, inspiring, and *intimidating* he could be, all at the same time. He wasn't a hair over five foot eight, and he was fifty-seven years old on that day I was scheduled to meet with him. Any six-foot-four, three-hundred-pound offensive lineman on the team would have had the good sense to be scared to death, but I was too dumb and maybe even a little too full of myself to know what I was walking into.

The staff member was waiting for me there in the conference room, along with the athletic director, the head trainer, and a few other administrators. And Bo himself.

"Coach," the staff member said, "this is Greg Harden."

I thanked everyone in the room and sat down. The staff member tried to open the conversation about the issue of substance abuse, but Bo cut him off. He delivered a diatribe that I'll politely call "old school" about zero tolerance and the dangers of coed dorms (yes, coed dorms!) and how the players just need somebody to hit them between the eyes with a good hard lecture about just saying no.

It was my turn to talk now. If you never had the chance to be stared down by a scowling Bo Schembechler, let me tell you, it's something you would never forget for the rest of your life. But I had already refused his initial request, had dragged everyone into this meeting, and now I had to figure out a way to tell one of the most iconic coaches in the country that his whole approach to dealing with a serious team issue was completely wrong.

"Coach," I said, "that's certainly one way to look at it."

He gave me a little smile—acknowledging that I could have challenged him but chose not to, that I didn't have to make him wrong for me to be right—and he sat back in his chair.

I launched into my pitch. "Say I give the speech," I said. "Just say no, don't ruin your life, end of story, amen. What happens next? One of your players self-identifies as someone who's already got a problem with drugs or alcohol, where's he going to go? You just told him there's zero tolerance, so why would he ever raise his hand?"

I went on to explain the contamination effect that a serious substance abuse problem can have on other members of the team. Somebody's getting drunk or getting high every weekend, you think they're doing it by themselves? And how will you ever find out about a problem before it's way too late? By the time *you* hear about it, it's probably out of control. The police are already involved; players are being taken away in handcuffs. Maybe there's a serious car accident, with innocent people hurt. It doesn't just affect the individual; it affects the entire team, the entire university.

"*Prevention* is just the first step," I said. "The second step is *intervention*, setting up a comprehensive program where athletes can safely come forward and get help. And the last step is *retention*, bringing athletes back into the program after they've taken responsibility for their mistakes. These are human beings we're talking about, coach. Seventeen- to twenty-two-year-old kids."

The room was silent again as Bo considered this. Then he said, "How do we make this happen?"

Flash forward to a couple of weeks later. I've helped the university set up a comprehensive intervention program, and now I'm standing in front of the entire football team. Coach Schembechler introduces me, tells the team who I am and how I'm starting a program for any of the players who feel that they need help with drugs or alcohol—or anything else. Coach spends another minute reading the team the riot act about how they need to pay attention, focus, listen to every word I say, and so on. Then he finally turns the meeting over to me.

"Thank you, Coach," I said. "I appreciate that introduction. Now, if you'll be kind enough, I would like you to leave the room."

Coach didn't hesitate. He already knew I was going to ask him to leave, because I made a point of telling him I would do that. But to the players . . . what a hell of a surprise!

Coach gave his team one more stern look and told them to remember what he had said about listening to me. And then he left.

I turned to the players, looked at their bewildered faces—they'd never seen anything like this before. "Tell me what just happened?"

What had happened was *trust*. It runs through this entire story. I trusted my own judgment, trusted that I knew the right way to approach this problem, and held my ground when I was put on the spot.

More importantly, Coach Schembechler made a huge statement when he put me in front of his football team and then left the room. That statement was *I trust this man, and I trust that he'll do the right thing for my team.*

This was coming from the man who put his team above everything else. "No man is more important than the Team," he said in a speech that has been repeated thousands of times at the university and beyond. "No coach is more important than the Team. *The Team, the Team, the Team.* And if we think that way, all of us, everything that you do, you take into consideration what effect does it have on my Team?"

What an incredible message to come from anyone who leads *any* kind of team. When your coach, your manager, your president—whoever is leading you—puts their *trust* in you to do what's best for the whole team, that's the most positive and empowering message they could ever send to you.

Without that kind of trust, I probably never would have worked in athletics at all. My whole life would have gone down a different road. But instead, I worked with Bo for the four years he was still at Michigan. He died in 2000, the night before the Michigan–Ohio State game.

I'll always remember Bo. And I'll always be grateful for his trust.

CHAPTER 16

THE TWO KINDS OF LOVE

I want to share with you a personal story from my life.

When my son Brian was fourteen years old, he was living with his mother in California. I was looking forward to the day when he would move out to live with me in Michigan. I thought that since he had grown up mostly with his mother, a little more male role modeling would be the right thing for him. So the plan was to make that happen when he turned fifteen.

Of course, you know what they say about plans. I remember the day Brian's mother called me and said, "You have to take him now."

"Why is that?" I asked.

"Because if you don't, I'm going to kill him."

If you've had a fourteen-year-old in the house, you might be able to relate to this. For me, this was all new. But ready or not, Brian came to live with me in Michigan. Suddenly, I was a single parent, and I had to rearrange my life quickly to adjust to this. But I was determined to make it work. I was committed to giving Brian a good, structured life so that I could help him develop into a man that his mother and I could be proud of.

It was a challenge for both of us. We had to really get to know each other. But we sorted it all out, and within a few months we had worked out a routine. Brian would get up and go to high school; I would go to work. I would come home just in time to meet him there. Then dinner, homework. Get to bed and do it again the next day. That's what our life looked like.

But then one day . . . And I remember this day like it just happened. The school bus came by; the door opened. A few kids got out.

But no Brian.

This may have happened once or twice before, but in those cases I knew that Brian was staying after school for some reason, and some arrangement had been made for him to get a ride home. Today, I didn't know anything about that, so I was a little irritated. I thought, he's going to hear about this as soon as he gets home.

Four o'clock. I'm even more irritated.

Four thirty. Now I'm steamed. This was before we all carried cell phones, mind you, but if he was at school or at a friend's house, he could still find a phone somewhere and call me.

Five o'clock. I'm furious.

Five thirty. I am absolutely *ballistic*. I am ready to kick this young man's butt the second he finally walks through that door.

At five forty-five—I remember the exact minute this happened—everything changed inside me. I started to feel something I had *never* experienced before. Every bad thing I could possibly imagine—it all filled up my head at once. Every possibility. I pictured him getting jumped into a gang. Or riding in the backseat of a car, on the way to some serious trouble.

Or lying dead in the street.

Or . . . Do I even have to say this? A fourteen-year-old Black male, anywhere in America. *Anywhere.* How could I *not* imagine him being in the wrong place at the wrong time, or doing something innocent that a white police officer nevertheless misconstrues as something warranting a sudden and violent response?

In that moment, it all hit me at once: this wasn't just a good young man who might occasionally need a little guidance and correction.

This was my *child*.

This was my *flesh and blood*.

This was *the love of my life*.

I knew in that moment that if something bad had really happened to him, my heart would be *shattered*. My life would be *destroyed*.

I had never felt such anguish before. And it lasted for the longest fifteen minutes of my life. An eternity. But then, at six o'clock, Brian walked through the door.

I was so overcome with relief, the anger I had been feeling just evaporated. I knew it had to be a big surprise to him, because he was probably expecting the hurricane as he walked through that door. And instead, he got a big hug from a man with tears in his eyes.

You'll have to forgive me if it sounds as if I was catching up to one of life's basic truths here. If you're a mother, you already know exactly what I was feeling. If you're a mother, you carried a life inside you for nine months, and then every moment since that child was born—every single moment—you feel an amazing, powerful connection. If anything ever threatens that connection, even for a second, you feel that, too, in a way that most men can't even understand. That's a mother's love. That's *God's love*. Unconditional and all-pervading.

For a father, it's usually something a little different. The love is conditional. Or at least, it *feels* that way. *This is who I want you to be. And then I'll love you.*

That was the love I had been giving to Brian. I had parceled it out with great care and determination. *Here's the program, son. Here's how you become the young man I will love.*

Until that moment, when I finally had the chance to feel the "other" kind of love. The love of a mother. The kind of love you *give away*, expecting nothing in return.

That's what Brian B. Harden taught me that day.

We may be talking about stereotypes here—the unconditional love of a mother and the conditional love of a father—but the distinction is real. (It certainly felt real to me in my relationship with my parents!) And understanding this difference has had a profound effect on my life and on my work.

Brian helped me to understand both kinds of love and to try to combine them in the best possible way: *I love you no matter what. But at the same time, we live in the real world and there always has to be some accountability.*

I learned to get past my expectations of what I wanted Brian to be. How he should think, what he should be doing in his life. I learned to love and accept him for exactly who he is. (And he has become an amazing adult, by the way, and has done so many things that I could never have imagined.)

These same ideas have also helped me become a better counselor and consultant. It doesn't matter if I'm trying to help a student athlete or a high-level professional executive—there is a basic need that *everyone* has:

Everyone wants to feel loved. Everyone wants to be accepted for who they are.

In "Chapter 6: What Does Success Look Like?" we talked about how people meet this basic need for love and acceptance in whatever way they can make it happen—whether those means are healthy or unhealthy.

Whether you're a parent, a counselor, or a leader of any kind at all, recognizing this need is one of the most powerful tools you can use to get the best from the people around you.

You can open that door by seeing each person for who they really are. As a whole person, not just an athlete or a businessperson or a child who carries your name. When you do that, when you *start* by giving them the love and acceptance that they really need, that's when you can help that person become the very best person he or she can be. With or without a particular sport, with or without a title or a six-figure income. With or without *anything* that you or anyone else might be expecting from them.

When these two kinds of love come together, it's the most powerful gift you can ever give!

CHAPTER 17

GET OUT OF YOUR OWN WAY!

Cooper Marody was a great hockey player for Michigan. He was the Big Ten scoring champion for the 2017–18 season, scored the game-winning goal in the NCAA regional semifinals that year, then another goal in the regional finals to help the team advance to the Frozen Four.

When his rights were traded to the Edmonton Oilers, Cooper left Michigan one year early to play on their farm team in the AHL. He got a brief call-up with the Oilers, not only fulfilling his dream of playing in the NHL, but wearing the same jersey that Wayne Gretzky once wore.

When he went back down to the AHL, he led his team in scoring and was named to the AHL All-Star team. As I write this, I know he'll be back on NHL ice next season.

But the Cooper Marody who is now living out his hockey dreams is not the Cooper Marody who first came into my office in 2016.

In some ways, Cooper's story reminds me a little of Tom Brady's. In fact, it was Cooper who asked his coach, Red Berenson, to make the appointment with me. Cooper had just watched the documentary *Inside the Mind of Tom Brady*. He had heard Tom talk about his struggles in his first season at Michigan—how he almost quit the team and went home, until the day he sat down in my office and I told him that none of the coaches would believe in him until he started to believe in himself.

Actually, Cooper's situation wasn't even as seemingly hopeless as Tom's was. He had already overcome much just to be sitting in my chair—this kid who was never considered big enough or fast enough to be a star on any level of the game. He had played two years in the juniors before coming to college, as many hockey players do. He had to endure being snubbed by the junior team that had drafted him—they drafted Cooper as a high school player but then changed their mind and didn't even invite him to their training camp! He had to go find a different junior team closer to home, beg his way onto the ice, and prove that he belonged. When he came to Michigan, he had a very good season for a freshman, playing in 32 games and scoring 10 goals and 14 assists.

But then he contracted mononucleosis and missed some classes because he was literally too exhausted to get out of bed, and because of that, the NCAA ruled him ineligible for the first part of his sophomore season. The team was struggling that year, and all Cooper could do was sit on the bench and watch it. By the time he got back on the ice, he had missed seventeen games, and Cooper started pressing in a way he had never done before. He played tight, overthinking every move on the ice. His body was healed, but his mind was not.

That's when he came to see me.

When I asked him why he was in my office, he unloaded.

All he ever wanted to do was play hockey for Michigan, but now, after having to sit out half a season and watch his team lose games, he wasn't sure he could ever be the same player again. Every time he got on the ice now, he was skating with fear—with the voices of self-doubt and self-recrimination screaming at him.

It didn't help that every time he made a mistake, he was getting the famous "stare" from Coach Berenson. It's a look that everyone who ever played for him can tell you about, just as every football player can tell you about the same kind of look from Bo Schembechler.

For the first time in Cooper's life, he wasn't enjoying the game. In fact, it was making him miserable.

He didn't know if he belonged here anymore—if he even belonged in the sport of hockey anymore. And he was pretty sure Coach Berenson was having the same doubts.

"I don't care what your coach thinks about you," I said. "He's gotten into your head, and now you're trying too hard to be perfect."

"But he makes me feel like—"

"He doesn't *make* you feel anything," I said. "He can say things to you, try to make you feel a certain way. But ultimately, how you feel is up to you."

(Sound familiar? Are the controllables being controlled here?)

I let him think about that for a moment, and then I asked him the most important question of all: "What was the greatest game you ever played?"

That surprised him.

"In your entire life," I said. "Pick the one game you think was your best, and tell me all about it."

He'd been playing ever since he was old enough to stand on two skates, so he had to take a moment to think back on it.

"It's hard to pick just one," he finally said. "But there was a string of games I played when I was at Sioux Falls, at the end of that season and into the championship."

It was his second year in the juniors. He was eighteen years old and had just been traded from the Muskegon Lumberjacks—the team he'd had to convince to let him play—to the Stampede in Sioux Falls, South Dakota. His first time living out of state, suddenly playing in the biggest arena in the USHL.

"Why were those your best games?" I asked him.

"I don't know. I guess I felt like I really hit my stride there. Everything I did on the ice, it just seemed to turn out right."

"Were you having fun?"

He smiled at the memory. "Yeah, I was. It was the best time I ever had playing hockey."

"And during these games, what were you thinking?"

He stopped cold this time. He just looked at me.

"Tell me what you were thinking during those games," I said.

He finally said: "Nothing."

"You were thinking *nothing*," I said. "And you were having *fun*?"

He hesitated, then said, "Yes."

"Because you were playing a *game*," I said. "A game that you *love*. That's all it was then. There was nothing else going on inside your head. And guess what. *You were the best player on the ice*."

That was the most important lesson Cooper needed to learn that day: he had to learn how to get out of his head. He had to remember how to *stay out of his own way* in order to be successful, both on and off the ice.

"There's only one reason why you're not having fun playing hockey right now," I told him. "It's because you *decided* not to have fun anymore. So the next time you practice, I want you to deliberately and intentionally decide that *nobody* is going to have more fun than you. In *practice*! I want you to piss everybody off because you're having so much fun. Because what are you doing when you're out there on that ice?"

"Playing a game," he said.

"That's right. So get out of your own head and go *play*."

The next weekend, the Michigan Wolverines took the ice against the Ohio State Buckeyes, and Cooper Marody scored his first-ever hat trick (three goals) as a collegiate hockey player.

He came back and had a great junior season, was named first team Big Ten, and led the league in scoring with 16 goals and 35 assists. I was sorry to see him leave a year early, but that's how it goes when the NHL calls. I still keep in touch with Cooper, talk to him whenever we both get a chance. Besides being a great player, he's also a great person. He's a talented musician (he released his first single in the summer of 2019), he's a devoted Christian, and he dares to stand out as a person who always makes the right choices in his life, even when he's surrounded by hockey players. (If you've met many hockey players, you know what I'm talking about. They often lead "colorful" lives when they're off the ice.) Cooper's life is what I like to call "faith-based and solution-focused." (That's my personal motto, a G-Harden original!)

Now that Cooper is playing at the highest levels of professional hockey, I can sometimes sense that he's pressing again, trying too hard to impress his coaches, trying too hard to be perfect. *Thinking* about the game instead of just *playing* it.

But I can always take him back to that first day in my office.

"Get out of your own head," I'll say to him. *"Stay out of your own way."*

I'm asking you to stop for a moment and think about your own life. How often are you . . .

- . . . your own worst enemy?
- . . . overthinking?
- . . . worrying about how other people see you?
- . . . beating yourself up?
- . . . worrying about things you can't change?
- . . . dragging around yesterday's baggage and feeling sorry for yourself?

Does any of this sound familiar?

I'm asking you to learn how to *get out of your own way*. Look yourself in the mirror, and be honest with yourself about what's holding you back.

This will only increase your commitment to the ultimate mission: Learn how to CONTROL THE CONTROLLABLES. Practice, train, and rehearse controlling your own thoughts and actions.

If you can't do it by yourself, seek help from a professional or from somebody you really trust. Give them permission to tell you the truth—because they can probably see quite clearly what you can't see for yourself. Let them help you push past those internal barriers that are sabotaging your happiness and keeping you from realizing your full potential.

Commit to staying out of your own way. And recommit to it, every single day.

RECOMMIT EVERY DAY

TO STAYING OUT OF

YOUR OWN WAY

—GREG HARDEN

COOPER MARODY

TESTIMONIAL

Cooper Marody played three seasons for the Michigan hockey team. As a junior, he was First Team All-Big Ten and led the league in scoring. He is currently playing at the professional level in the Edmonton Oilers organization. Also a talented musician, he released his first single in 2019.

"Although hockey is what I do, it is not who I am."

Greg Harden was a massive influence in my life. I always admired Tom Brady because he was a sixth-round draft pick and I was a sixth-round draft pick. He went to Michigan as an underdog, and I did, too. One day I was watching a video on YouTube called *Inside the Mind of Tom Brady*. In the video, Tom talked about how much Greg helped him. And Greg talked about working with Tom and what he saw in him. What Greg had to say was so inspiring to me, that literally the next day, I asked Coach Berenson if he could set up a meeting for me with Greg.

When I got to Greg's office, I was fired up and anxious to hear what he had to say. The video had inspired me, but even more, I was *ready* to hear his message. This all came about at a time when I was having some doubts about myself as a hockey player. I was putting my whole self-worth into hockey, and this mindset was holding me back in hockey and in life.

Greg explained to me that his job with Tom Brady was not to make him a great football player. Not at all. His job with Tom Brady was to convince him that with or without football, he was going to do something great with his life. This was the message that really resonated with me. I wanted the same thing. I wanted Greg to convince me that with or without hockey, I was going to do something great.

It was my lifelong dream to go to the University of Michigan and play hockey. Instead of enjoying it, at times I was miserable. There were days I *hated* going to the rink. I was putting so much pressure on myself to be successful, and if I wasn't, my self-worth suffered greatly. If I had a bad game, I berated and doubted myself. This caused me to lose confidence in myself as a player and as a person.

Greg was able to pull me out of this mindset. He helped me to see that I, like many athletes, am a perfectionist, with a fear of failure. He helped me see that if I go to the rink each day and give 100 percent, and it still doesn't work out, then it wasn't *supposed* to work out. The only thing I can control is the effort I put into it, and the rest would take care of itself. Greg helped me turn what had become my worst attribute back into my *best* attribute. Instead of getting caught up and worrying about always trying to be perfect, Greg helped me channel that energy in a way that prevented me from becoming my own worst enemy.

Greg helped me to appreciate that never being satisfied and always wanting more is good attribute to have if managed correctly. He helped me to allow myself to enjoy my successes and to give myself a little credit for them. He also showed me that it's okay to fail. What matters is what you learn from it and how you respond. This helped me to not only be a better hockey player, but to enjoy life that much more. Greg always reminded me that hockey is just a game. If I'm going to get paid for doing something I love, then so be it. Take that deal! But never forget, it's a game that you play because you love it. This mindset has taken the mental handcuffs off and given me the confidence to go to levels in hockey that I could never have imagined.

Another thing that Greg helped me understand is that "outliers" do things differently. I never drank in college. Sometimes that commitment made it hard to fit in. I look back on that now and I am proud of my decision, but at the time, I didn't value the good choices I was making or the person I was. I mostly valued my success in hockey. Greg helped me to not only keep making the right choices, but to embrace those choices. He taught me to love being an outlier.

At the end of my first season as a pro, I had to deal with a serious injury. Thankfully, I got through it. But it did make me ask myself: If hockey is taken away from me, am I going to be okay with myself? Would my life still be great?

This is the most important thing I learned from Greg. If God took away my ability to play hockey and I could never put on the gear again, my self-worth would be okay. I would still live a great life! Why? Because hockey does not define my worth. Greg helped me see that although hockey is what I do, it is not who I am.

CHAPTER 18

SWOT YOURSELF

Let me share with you a quick story about one of the athletes I once worked with—a young woman at Michigan who was struggling with low self-confidence and what I call extreme "negative self-talk." The amazing thing was that she was probably the best player on her team, with all the stats and all the awards to prove it. Yet she was still obsessed with finding fault with herself.

We worked hard to find the roots of this obsession. Why did she never see the positive in herself? Only the negative. "Beating yourself up all the time doesn't work," I said. "Unless it's your *mission* to be miserable, negative, and depressed."

The days turned into weeks, and we couldn't break through, couldn't find any kind of trigger from her past. In fact, her life was like a storybook. Great parents. Amazing, supportive coaches.

"Okay," I said to her one day. "It's time to do a SWOT analysis."

"What's that?" she asked.

"S-W-O-T," I said. "You're going to examine your *strengths* and your *weaknesses*. Then you're going to think about what kind of woman you want to become, and you'll look at your *opportunities* to get there, as well as the *threats* that stand in your way. It's a great way to become an expert on *who you are*, and the process you need to follow to become that person *you want to be*."

I had her take a sheet of paper and draw a vertical line down the middle, and a horizontal line right across the middle, dividing the page into four quadrants:

In the top left, I had her put a capital "S" for "strengths," where she would write down her skills, her good attitudes, the behaviors she exhibited that were really working for her.

In the top right, a "W" for "weaknesses." The skills she didn't have yet, the attitudes that weren't so good, the behaviors that clearly were *not* working.

In the lower left, "O" for "opportunities." Networks she had already built, the supportive people in her life, the favorable circumstances in which she may have found herself.

Then finally, in the lower right, "T" for "threats." The negatives forces and obstacles, external or internal, that stood in her way on the path to becoming her ideal self.

(See "Worksheet: SWOT Analysis" on page 119, and do your own!)

I had her start by making her list in each category. No surprise to me, she had a hard time identifying her strengths, but did she ever go to town on her weaknesses! I thought she did a better-than-average job identifying the opportunities and threats in her life, but I kept coming back to that first category. She literally didn't know her own strengths!

So I asked her to take the whole process a step further. I had her identify two or three people in her life, whom she loved and respected, to fill in those squares with their own independent and objective lists, written entirely from their perspectives. I wanted to make sure that she chose people who were capable of giving their honest opinions, "straight with no chaser," but at the same time thoughtful and caring enough not to abuse this trust. You want to be able to see things through their eyes that you might not be able to see with your own.

She ended up choosing her mother and her head coach. When we looked at the SWOTs produced for her by those two important people in her life, it was striking to me just how similar a portrait they both drew, working completely independently.

But no surprise, she went right past the strengths and zeroed in on the weaknesses they listed. "Yep, that's right," she said to each point. Weakness by weakness, she validated every single one. "They know me better than anybody."

"Now go back to the strengths," I said. "What did they say?"

She couldn't even read them out loud. "They just felt obligated to write *something*," she said. "So they made these up."

"Don't you find it interesting," I said, "that they both made up the same things? What are the odds?"

She didn't try to answer. I kept going.

"So in your opinion," I said, "both of these people were dead-on accurate in listing all your weaknesses, but they were completely incapable of coming up with any genuine strengths?"

"I'm not saying that," she stammered. "It's just that they care about me. They couldn't just leave that section blank."

I took the papers from her. "You would have said the same thing about *anyone* who did this for you, and about any strength they listed, no matter how many times they all agreed. And I'm not going to buy it anymore."

She just looked at me.

"It's one or the other," I said. "Either you trust in both the negative and the positive, or you don't trust any of it at all. What's it going to be?"

That choice she had to make was the start of a major shift in her thinking. She finally had to deal with her negative self-image and try to discover where it had come from.

I've used the same SWOT technique with countless other people I've worked with. The original idea came from a presentation I was asked to give to a group of executives who would come back to Michigan's business school for continuing education. If you live in that world, you may already be familiar with a SWOT analysis as applied to a business. So why not use the same analysis on yourself? Treat yourself as if you were a business; then systematically and scientifically gather this data on your own strengths and weaknesses, as well as the opportunities for success and the threats that might get in your way. In the end, it's as if you're asking yourself, *If I were a business, would someone want to invest in my future?*

In gathering this input, it can get very interesting—and usually very revealing—when I ask them to go find those opinions from other people in their life. I remember a young man who was an assistant to a state politician, who went out and got SWOTs from a boss who had fired him, and a woman who had broken up with him. I didn't tell him at the time, but I thought he was taking a huge risk. He was obviously confident about their character and the commitment they had to him.

When we went over the SWOTs the next week, you can imagine just how detailed and poignant those reviews were. But can anyone deny that this man was dead serious about getting honest feedback?

I encourage you to give this critical self-assessment tool a try sometime. But when I say "critical self-assessment," please don't confuse that with being overly self-critical, like that young woman who could see only the negatives about herself and none of the positives. The four quadrants on the page are all equally sized for a reason.

Be honest about both your strengths and your weaknesses, and then keep going with the opportunities for success and the threats that must be overcome. In the end, it's really quite simple. All you're doing is trying to find out what's working in your life—and what's *not* working.

You'll be amazed at the insights this tool can reveal. And then even more amazed when you ask two or three people close to you for their honest input, to see through their eyes what you might not see through your own.

Who will you select?

WORKSHEET
SWOT ANALYSIS

STRENGTHS	**W**EAKNESSES
OPPORTUNITIES	**T**HREATS

CHAPTER 19

COMMIT, IMPROVE, MAINTAIN

It's Friday morning. I'm on my way to a small town about ninety miles away, to talk to a group of young people. They're anywhere from twelve to eighteen years old, and they've all been labeled "high risk." Most come from broken homes, surrounded by drug and alcohol abuse. Many of them have already been through the legal system and are highly likely to return. I'm realistic enough to know that one talk from me is not going to transform them into a room full of high achievers. But maybe, just maybe, if I can just get through to one or two of these kids, I can make a difference.

But what am I going to say?

I think back on the week I've just had. On Monday morning, I met with a group of high-performance athletes and helped them focus on their goal of making the Olympics. On Monday afternoon, I was the invited speaker at a discussion group that included a major city's mayor, its superintendent of public schools, board members from several large corporations, PhDs, sociologists, psychiatrists, a nationally renowned social activist, and leaders from several religious and fraternal organizations.

On Tuesday morning, I met with one of the university athletic teams, to help them prepare for a run at a national championship. In the afternoon, I had individual counseling sessions with players from four different sports. In the evening, I conducted a workshop for prison inmates—and brought along with me several young men to expose them to this environment, in the hope that they'd see the fate that awaits any man who does not master his mind, his decisions, his emotions, and ultimately his behavior.

I spent all of Wednesday training managers at a Fortune 100 company on the topic "Managing the Troubled Employee."

On Thursday morning, I was back to individual counseling, helping one athlete develop a peak-performance mindset, helping another athlete with a potential eating disorder, and helping yet another athlete determine whether his depression was episodic or a chronic mental health problem. I ended the morning in a meeting with the concerned parents and the coach of another troubled athlete. On Thursday afternoon, I led a seminar on "Self-Defeating Attitudes and Behaviors" with a group of recovering addicts at a methadone clinic.

That was my week so far. Now it's Friday morning, and I'm on my way to face this group of high-risk kids, and when I reflect on my week and think about the meetings, the interviews, and the presentations, there's one common theme on a universal truth. Whether the person hearing it is a prison inmate, a recovering addict, an athlete training for the Olympics or competing for a national title, a manager or board member of a major corporation, a school's superintendent, or a mayor, they all want the same thing.

They want their lives to be better.

The words I use might be a little different, the sense of urgency may be more acute for some than for others, but the basic message doesn't change.

"Every one of you is standing at a crossroads," I begin. "If you want to make your life better, you have to make a *commitment*. That's number one. Number two, you have to *improve* your own performance, in everything you do. And number three, you have to make a plan to *maintain* that performance over time."

Commit.

Improve.

Maintain.

I ask each of these young people to consider, just for a moment, how much they have in common with all the other people I've worked with this week. No matter how many trials they've faced or how much trouble they've endured, no matter how much soaring success or abject failure they've experienced, they all just want their lives to work better.

And along the way toward making that dream come true, every single one of those people—inmate, addict, athlete, or CEO—faced the same kind of fear, the same kind of self-doubt. We all have this in common, every single one of us here on this earth.

Commit.

Improve.

Maintain.

The first step, *commit*, is essential and often overlooked. "Yeah, of course I want a better life. Who doesn't?"

No. Stop right where you are. Don't just say those words and move on.

Stop yourself right now and do this right. Start by asking yourself these questions:

What's important to me?

What do I want to achieve in my life?

What improvements do I have to make to reach that goal?

Commit. Right now. Commit to making those improvements.

Okay, now that you've done that, you can start thinking about how you're going to start making those changes. In class, at home, in your relationships, at work and at play. Begin making those changes, one at a time. *Improve.*

Keep going. Today. Tomorrow. Never stop.

Maintain.

Consistency is the key to achieving that goal. Maintain those positive changes. Maintain your peak performance. If you do this, *I promise you*, there are no limits to what you can accomplish.

Commit.

Improve.

Maintain.

This is what will take you to the next level, what will propel you to reach that milestone you once thought impossible. To overcome adversity, to recover from that injury or that addiction. To stay out of prison, go back to school, advance your career, build your income, or accomplish whatever goal you have for yourself.

It will transform your behavior.

It will transform your mindset.

It will transform your *life*.

COMMIT

IMPROVE

MAINTAIN

—GREG HARDEN

JONATHAN SATOVSKY,

Founder and CEO, Satovsky Asset Management

TESTIMONIAL

A Michigan graduate, Jonathan Satovsky heard secondhand accounts of Greg's impact on the lives of several student athletes and decided to learn everything he could about this man, finally getting the chance to meet him in 2018. He is the founder and CEO of Satovsky Asset Management in New York.

"You were coaching me before you even knew me."

The way I stumbled upon Greg Harden was having been born in Ann Arbor and being a Michigan fan for my entire life. It's hard to understand how powerful it is if you don't grow up in an environment like this. And being a part of that has brought me so many different moments in my life: friendships, successes, failures, drama. So as I go along with the rest of my life, my attention keeps getting pulled back to Michigan, and Michigan sports. And I stumbled upon the *60 Minutes* piece with Greg Harden, particularly the interview they did with Tom Brady, and being in finance, you learn all about due diligence and how to dig deeper than most people to find the real truth that lies underneath. I've learned over the years the importance of doing that, because as I've gotten closer to certain role models in my life, when I dig a little deeper, I often end up finding things that are dismaying to me, and I've become a little jaded over the years with some of these "false idols."

But the more I learned about Greg Harden, the more I was determined to meet him. So I happened to be at this Michigan event, and a friend of mine knew I'd been talking about Greg Harden and he told me that he was there at the event! I walked over to him as he was finishing a conversation with someone else. I put my arm around him, and he's looking at me like, who the hell are you? I told him, "I just wanted to express my gratitude to you for the great effect you've had on my life in the past few years, even from afar. You transformed my life as a father, as a business owner, as a coach, as a leader, as a friend, as someone who tries to aspire to be a better version of himself every day. And I just wanted to thank you for being a role model and a mentor and an inspiration in all of the things you're doing for the University of Michigan, helping these kids achieve things they otherwise wouldn't have achieved. But also, the ripple effect you've had, like dropping a pebble in a lake, transcends the university and half a million alums across the Michigan tribe. And that ripple effect from the lives you've touched keeps rolling outward, touching untold numbers of people you haven't even met. Helping people be a force for positivity, be a force for change, be a force for leadership."

"Leaders and Best" is what Michigan stands for, and Greg Harden stands for that more than anyone else I've ever met.

I've learned so much about coaching in the past few years, and I have a real obsession with learning everything I can about it. One idea I've learned is that just a 1 percent change can make such a huge difference in your life over time. I think Greg's magic is the subtlety of knowing how to get someone, with no bullshit, with total candor, to just see how a small shift in their perspective, in their attitude, can have such a big effect. Just letting that small shift sink in, letting them practice it, and then seeing how their life changes. See how Desmond Howard goes from wanting to quit the team to becoming a Heisman winner. How Tom Brady goes from fourth-stringer, feeling despondent and thinking about going back home, to becoming one of the best players who ever played the game. He bought into the subtle change in his mindset and his attitude, and he had someone who would hold him accountable for that.

In sports, you always have a clear winner and loser. The game ends and you look at the scoreboard. In life, it's not always that easy to tell if you're winning or losing. In my own industry, there may be a scoreboard that shows you how much money you've made—and I'll be the first to admit that I once had that stupid poster that said, "He who has the most toys wins"—but I know that's not the right scoreboard. Greg has helped me see that success in life, and showing up for the people that you love, and being present and enthusiastically engaged in every moment, *is* winning.

The world needs to come together to communicate in an optimistic, healthier way, to make things not about me, me, me, but about *we*. How can we, together, do things in everyone's best interest, not how can I do something where I win and you lose. In the world, it doesn't have to be a game of win and lose. Everyone can win.

If everyone showed up with more of an open mind and an open heart, like Greg tries to teach . . . If a Tom Brady or a Desmond Howard can show up in the way that Bo Schembechler talked about, where it's all about the Team, and if you can trust that your teammates have your back and you have theirs and that you can build that team and that culture and that community so that everyone is working in sync rather than having that need to look better than other people on the team . . . Those lessons are so deeply rooted, beyond sports, to every aspect of life, whether it's a family or a marriage or a business or a country. That idea transcends everything.

CHAPTER 20

HOW TO CREATE BAD HABITS . . . AND GOOD ONES

When I was a younger man, I had a real problem talking to people. (If you know me now, you're laughing, but it's true. I'm a natural-born introvert!) It was especially hard for me to talk to complete strangers.

Another thing I had a real problem with: conflict. I would do just about anything to avoid it or defuse it.

So whenever I went out of town, I would intentionally try this experiment on myself: I would make myself approach strangers, both men and women. I would make myself engage in small talk. I would make myself stand up for myself, even if it caused conflict. As long as I was in a strange place, where nobody knew me and nobody would ever see me again, I was free to try on this whole new personality. I would make a *game* out of it. A competition with myself.

I was using this game to train myself to be comfortable talking to strangers and to train myself to be assertive. I didn't necessarily have to seek out conflict, but I didn't have to bend over backward avoiding it, either. I knew that these would be good habits to have, to make my life better.

When we're talking about self-defeating attitudes and behaviors ("Chapter 7: The Demon on Your Left Shoulder: Self-Defeating Attitudes and Behaviors") and self-supporting attitudes and behaviors ("Chapter 8: The Angel on Your Right Shoulder: Self-*Supporting* Attitudes and Behaviors"), it may be helpful to look at many of these as pure *habits* that we've picked up over the years.

If you have the *habit* of negative self-talk, for instance—always criticizing yourself, always expecting the least from yourself—stop and ask yourself, how did this become a habit? It became a habit because it's something that you've done repeatedly and consistently over time. Do anything enough times, and it's going to become natural. It's going to become a part of you. It's going to become a *habit*.

So turn it around. If this is how you create a *bad* habit, doesn't it make sense that you can use the same method to create a *good* habit? Or better yet, that you could take that bad habit of yours and *replace* it with a good habit? That you could even make the bad habit *trigger* the good habit?

It's not going to happen overnight, but think about how you could make this work. You start by studying yourself. Become a social scientist, with yourself as the subject. Watch to see how often this bad habit arises. What specific circumstances in your life bring it out?

That's the first step: awareness. If it's a strong enough habit and you're watching carefully, you'll be amazed by how often you catch it.

The second step is key. Some people are totally oblivious to their habits. But others, when they see themselves indulging in a bad habit, will beat themselves up over it. Another bad habit laid over the first bad habit!

Instead of doing that, here's what I'm asking you to do: Be *amused* by it. Be *entertained* by it.

When you do that—when you learn to laugh at yourself instead of harming yourself over your bad habits—you have a much better chance to replace that habit with something better.

That's the third step. When you see the bad habit in yourself, when you've forgiven yourself and even allowed yourself to be amused and entertained by it, now you deliberately and intentionally decide what you're going to do instead:

- You're going to encourage yourself instead of tearing yourself down. (This extends to encouraging others and not tearing them down.)
- You're going to stand up for yourself instead of allowing yourself to be treated like a doormat. (This includes standing up for others.)
- You're going to react with patience instead of anger.

These are going to be your new habits.

It's going to feel fake at first. The first time, the first ten times, maybe the first hundred times. What's that old expression? *Fake it till you make it.* Give yourself permission to feel that way. And give yourself permission to fail. It's not always going to work, especially not at first.

But keep at it. Make these new habits a part of your life, and they'll become part of *you.*

And never forget, *simple* doesn't mean *easy.* As simple as this assignment is, it will require a serious commitment to change, to reinvent, to transform yourself. If you are convinced that you cannot do something, you will never even try. So be courageous enough to ask for help if you need it!

CHAPTER 21

IT'S PERFECTLY OKAY NOT TO BE PERFECT

When you work at a university that recruits the best of the best, you will be dealing with athletes who come from all over the world, with big dreams of stardom on and off the field, court, diamond, ice, track, you name it. You're going to meet a lot of young perfectionists.

They spend too much of their time and energy being *obsessed* with being perfect at everything they do. Often, gymnasts are at the top of my list in fitting this profile. From the time they're four years old, gymnasts are training to get a perfect 10 on every routine they perform. And if they're good enough to be doing it at the Division I level, they've probably received a few 10s along the way.

And not only did they have to stick a perfect landing, they had to do it with a big smile on their face! Talk about being perfect.

I can't tell you how many athletes and professionals I've worked with over the years who strive to be perfect and are absolutely *terrified* of failing. Of letting everyone down.

The baggage of being "practically perfect in every way," to quote a line from Mary Poppins, is heavy, and I've seen many young athletes struggle under this weight.

When I was learning how to be a counselor, one of the first things they taught was that *nobody is perfect* and that therefore, trying to be perfect can result only in disappointment.

It makes sense, right?

But I don't buy it.

That's right, I'm going off the script here.

Whenever I meet an obsessive perfectionist, the first thing I tell him or her is this: *Go ahead and try to be perfect.*

Get a 100 on that test.

Score a perfect 10 on the high bar.

It's fun to be perfect!

Just don't *expect* to be perfect. Don't *demand* to be perfect. Because that is a recipe for disaster.

See, I'm not telling anyone that perfectionism is bad. All I'm saying is that you have to have balance. You have to have harmony. You have to see yourself as a whole person. Positive and negative. Yin and yang. Chaos and order. You are all of these things, because you live in the real world.

You are a human being, and making mistakes is part of being human. If you demand something else—say, a perfectionism that no human can achieve—then you're sabotaging your own self-love and self-acceptance.

So try to go for 4-for-4 at the plate. Bat 1.000 for the game! Who wouldn't love that? But if all you have is negative self-talk every time you make a mistake, then every mistake you make will probably lead to *five more mistakes*, just because you're so busy beating yourself up. Worrying about being taken out of the game. Worrying about being judged. Worrying about not meeting your own impossibly high standards.

It doesn't work.

Beating yourself up does not work. Worrying does not work.

They are ineffective!

No matter where your perfectionism comes from—maybe you were raised this way, maybe you got it drilled into your head by some coach along the way, or maybe it was just a part of you from the day you were born—you have to teach yourself that your best chance of success comes when your perfectionism and your realism are in balance.

You can't be afraid of failure.

If you're afraid to fail, you are afraid to succeed.

Think back to when you were a child. When you were learning to ride a bike, throw a Frisbee, or do any of a hundred other things that seemed almost impossible when you first tried them. When you were four years old and your father let go of the bike, were you worried about looking bad?

No! You were only worried about falling. And you *did* hit the pavement. But then you got up and brushed yourself off and tried again. You may have failed a dozen times before you finally got it.

So . . . now that you're an adult, why are you so afraid to fail?

I don't want to look stupid. I don't want to be judged.

Just stop it. Knock it the hell off. Failure is part of life. You can't be overwhelmed by it. Grow. Evolve. See failure as an opportunity to learn what works and what doesn't work. And then recalibrate. Or start over.

You might stop having unrealistic expectations of yourself, and maybe of others who struggle to be accepted by you.

And stop worrying about letting other people down. Perfectionists get so preoccupied with this fear, they forget that those other people probably aren't even thinking about them, because they're too preoccupied with their own problems. When you worry so much about letting other people down, the person let down is usually just you.

But hey, I still love perfectionists! I'm *entertained* by them. If you're a perfectionist and I can teach you to be entertained by your obsession, to have *fun* with being a perfectionist instead of being overwhelmed by it . . .

Then I encourage you to *try* being perfect whenever you can. Because the *pursuit* of perfection (knowing it's not always attainable) can be awesome. Giving 100 percent, 100 percent of the time, win, lose, or draw—*that's* a healthy obsession.

IF YOU'RE AFRAID TO FAIL

YOU'RE AFRAID TO SUCCEED

—GREG HARDEN

CHAPTER 22

THE VALUE OF A SHORT MEMORY

There have been some great coaches at the University of Michigan. Bo Schembechler's football teams won thirteen Big Ten titles in twenty years. John Beilein took basketball teams at three other schools to the NCAA tournament before coming to Michigan and taking the Wolverines to two championship games in five years. And Red Berenson coached the hockey team for thirty-three years, with eleven appearances in the Frozen Four, and two NCAA championships.

But none of these coaches can match the record of Carol Hutchins. Not even close.

In thirty-five years of coaching the Michigan softball team, "Hutch" has more wins (over 1,500) than any other coach in any Michigan sport, men's or women's, and more than any other softball coach in NCAA history.

She is also—I am not kidding—one of the most formidable human beings I have ever met. If you put all our current coaches in a room, including Jim Harbaugh (six foot three, fourteen seasons in the NFL) and Juwan Howard (six foot nine, nineteen seasons in the NBA), it's Carol Hutchins who would probably walk out the door, brushing the dust from one shoulder.

Whenever Hutch calls me, I'm already saying to myself as I pick up the phone: *It's going to be a pitcher*. And most times, I'm right!

Because think about what a pitcher does. Baseball or softball, everything starts in the pitcher's head. That's literally every event in the entire game. Sure, the catcher can put down a sign beforehand, indicating the type of pitch and where it should go . . . but then everything goes into a state of anticipation.

The batter is waiting, the catcher is waiting, the fielders are waiting. Even the umpires and all the fans in the stadium are waiting.

They're waiting for one person to decide exactly when and how he or she will move from stillness into sudden, violent motion. Once that happens, everything else becomes reactive, but it all starts with that small voice in the pitcher's head saying, "*Go.*"

Whenever I talk to a softball pitcher who's in a funk and starting to seriously doubt herself, I start with one idea: *Let's look at the data.*

The data is all your history up until this point, all of the great games you've had, and the reasons why Coach Hutchins recruited you in the first place. The *data* proves to you that you're a capable, qualified, and competent athlete.

Unless you're really going to try to tell me the coach was wrong about you.

So now it's all about your *beliefs*. It's about how you *talk to yourself* when you're on the mound.

It's a great life lesson that goes well beyond softball or any other sport. It's all about how you treat yourself, how you talk to yourself, what you *believe* about yourself. You can't base your self-worth, your self-image, your self-esteem on what happens to a ball after you've thrown it. If the batter hits the ball 295 feet and the outfielder catches it, you're okay with yourself, but if the ball goes 300 feet and just clears the wall, now you're a worthless failure?

If that's really how you talk to yourself, you have to recalibrate!

You have to learn to let it go. To move on to the next pitch, or the next game, or the next season.

I'm not talking about becoming a robot. When you fail, it *hurts*. It really does. And it *should*! You should let yourself feel that.

I just gave up a home run and I'm *not happy*. I am going to acknowledge that this thing happened, and then I'm going to give myself *permission* to feel like crap about it.

For one-tenth of a second.

That's right, *one-tenth of a second*.

Hit the start button on the stopwatch. Feel like crap. Hit the stop button. 00:00.10.

Now get back to work. If there's something to learn from the mistake you just made, learn it. Make the adjustment. Hear the words in your head that reinforce your commitment to giving your best effort: *I'm capable, qualified, and competent.*

And then move on.

It's the one trait so many of the greatest athletes I've ever known have in common: *a short memory*. My shot doesn't go in. I drop the ball. I miss the wide-open net.

I give myself *one-tenth of a second* to feel bad, and then I keep playing.

It works the other way, too. The ball goes in, I catch the pass, I score the goal. Now I've got *one-tenth of a second* to feel great about it before I get back to the game.

To become a peak performer, you have to retrain, reprogram, re-engineer yourself not to obsess over "triumph and disaster" and learn (to quote Rudyard Kipling) to "treat those two impostors just the same."

I know, it's easy for me to tell a softball pitcher or any other athlete—hell, any other person in any walk of life—not to wallow in self-pity. To know the value of a short memory. To get over it and get on with it.

So sometimes, I'll take it a step further. For those of you who have been beating yourself up, getting down on yourself, feeling sorry for yourself . . .

How's that working for you?

I'm seriously asking. Is it helping you? Are you gaining some advantage from it? I mean, unless it's really your mission in life to be negative, miserable, and depressed, then STOP beating yourself up!

Because it's not working.

It's not helping.

It's *ineffective*.

So STOP doing it!

CHAPTER 23

A PERMANENT SOLUTION
TO A TEMPORARY PROBLEM

In my first job after grad school, I was working as a clinical therapist in a hospital. I had been there exactly two weeks and two days when the boss came up to me and said, "Greg, we had an overdose patient come into the ER last night. A young woman, fifteen years old, who attempted suicide. We've already had several of our counselors go up and try to talk to her, but they were all rejected. We had our senior counselor give it a try and that didn't go any better. So we sent the psychiatrist in to see her, and I'm afraid that didn't go very well at all. So finally, I decided to give it a try myself, and, um . . . well, quite frankly, I tried my best."

I kept nodding my head, listening carefully.

He cleared his throat and said, "Would you like to go see her and give it a try?"

Remember, I'd been on the job only two weeks and two days. What could I possibly say to this young woman that the others hadn't?

Hell no, I thought as I looked him straight in the eye and said, "Yes, sir, I'd be glad to."

You can imagine that elevator ride up to the fifth floor. The demons of despair, fear, and self-doubt all descended on me. "Fool, you've been here two weeks and two days," they said to me. "What are *you* going to do?"

But those demons forgot one thing: I had already decided that they were *predictable* and, therefore, *manageable*. (I'll talk more about this in "Chapter 25: Fear, Courage, and 'Buck Fever.'") I knew they'd show up, so I was prepared to dismiss them. Once I did that, I had ninety seconds to figure out my next move.

I got to the fifth floor, walked down to the young woman's room, straightened my tie, took a deep breath . . . and exploded into the room. I had a big smile on my face. I was giddy and excited, as if I could barely control my enthusiasm.

The young woman pulled the covers over her head.

It didn't even slow me down. "I'm so excited to meet you," I said. "I heard you were the most amazing human being, and I just had to come up and talk to you in person."

Nothing.

"The first young lady to ever play for the football team," I went on. "That's just so amazing. Tell me, are you a kicker? Are you a quarterback? What happened to you, anyway? Is your leg broken? We have a great orthopedic staff here, one of the best in the state."

The covers came down. The young woman poked her face out.

"I am *not* a football player," she said, seething. "I did *not* break my leg."

"Oh," I said, looking surprised. "Then who are you?"

"It doesn't matter," she said. "I don't want to talk to you."

"Why is that?"

"Because you're gonna say the same thing like everyone else who's walked into this room. I'm too young, I haven't thought about the rest of my life, I have so much to live for."

I changed my body language, changed my tone of voice, stepped up very close to her, and said, "Have I done *anything* like *anyone* you've met so far?"

She shrank back into her pillow. "No, sir," she said.

"Then don't tell me how I'm going to act and what I'm going to say."

"Yes, sir," she said.

"All right, so you want to tell me why you decided to take yourself out?"

That's how we engaged. She started to tell me her story. At the beginning, I was angry. By the end, I was sad. The story of this fifteen-year-old young woman's life broke my heart.

She was living with a twenty-seven-year-old addict who had introduced her to every drug imaginable. In the house were several other addicts, and this young woman was the one person responsible for taking care of the whole household—cooking, cleaning, and most importantly, going out every day to buy the drugs. On top of all this, her boyfriend was a paraplegic who required a tremendous amount of care. She had to feed him, clean him, clothe him every day, and in return he belittled her, demeaned her, made her feel worthless. Fifteen years old and this was her life—she was broken down, worn out, estranged from her own family, and mentally, physically, and perhaps sexually abused.

When she was done talking, I wiped away my tears and I said, "I understand."

She was surprised. "You do?"

"You're fifteen years old," I said, "and you just wanted the pain to stop. What other way out did you have?"

"Oh, thank you," she said. "Thank you for understanding."

"I may understand," I said, "but I don't agree with your strategy. You came up with a *permanent solution to a temporary problem.* Will you allow me to help you examine some other options?"

We began working together. In six months, this young woman transformed herself, and the ideas I shared with her were the same ideas I teach anyone else who comes into my life. In your darkest moment, you have to be willing to accept help from someone else, but ultimately, it's self-love and self-acceptance that are the critical pieces of the puzzle. Looking outside yourself for your own self-worth and your self-esteem will never work in the end.

I encouraged her to practice, train, and rehearse believing in herself. To trust herself. And to stop believing that just because someone *needs* you, they *love* you.

As I've said before . . .

Your best friend in the world has to be you.

CHAPTER 24:

FAITH-BASED AND SOLUTION-FOCUSED

In "Chapter 17: Get Out of Your Own Way!" I talk about a remarkable young hockey player. When Cooper began to feel like he was hating the game of hockey in his sophomore year, I challenged him to get back to the idea that it's a *game* and that he should be having *fun* playing it.

And because Cooper had made it clear to me that his faith was a huge part of his life, I felt comfortable asking him if he had faith every day of the week—not just Sunday.

"You cannot let hockey be an idol god," I said to him. "You cannot let the NHL be what you worship, or God will take it from you."

You don't say something like that lightly, not to someone like Cooper Marody, but he understood exactly what I was saying, and it helped him put the game in perspective.

The other remarkable thing about Cooper was that he was a college hockey player who didn't drink, use drugs, or engage in casual sex. Some would suggest he was an *outlier* in a group of eighteen- to twenty-three-year-old college hockey players.

The more I got to know and appreciate him, the more I could challenge him to accept being an outlier. To *love* being an outlier.

To love being that person who broke the stereotype about athletes in his sport.

And to love being a leader on his team, whom other players could look up to as a counterexample. You don't have to be a certain kind of person to play hockey. In fact, you can be a *great* player who just so happens to be FAITH-BASED AND SOLUTION-FOCUSED.

In "Chapter 5: Dream Big, Believe Big, Become Big," I described the three different types of fitness: physical, mental, and *spiritual*. "Spiritual" doesn't mean you have to believe in my religion or even my concept of God, but I believe it is vitally important that you believe in something bigger than yourself. Because there will come a time when your body is spent, your mind is broken, and yet you can still tap into something deeper, something that cannot be described or explained.

We've all seen it happen, in our own lives and in the lives of those around us—constant reminders of this deeper well of power. If you look carefully enough, you can see miracles every day.

Without telling you what to believe, I still want to encourage you to think about your spiritual fitness just as much as you pay attention to your physical and mental fitness. With all three in balance, you will truly be developing yourself, internally and externally.

Being FAITH-BASED AND SOLUTION-FOCUSED means that you have a belief system not limited by intellect or emotions.

It means you see yourself as more than just muscle and bone.

It means that even a true believer must participate and commit to solving problems with decisions and actions.

Cooper Marody was one of the best I've ever worked with at capturing this philosophy and making it work.

CHAPTER 25

FEAR, COURAGE, AND "BUCK FEVER"

I was working with a player on the baseball team, a pitcher who was struggling to manage his nerves. All the talent in the world, but he couldn't perform consistently when it mattered most.

We spent a long time talking it over, trying to find a way for him to live up to his potential. I suggested some breathing techniques to help him calm his nerves. I gave him some reading material on mindfulness. I asked him to increase his self-awareness and learn to control his own negative self-talk.

I tried every exercise in my arsenal, but nothing helped. When the game was on the line, he kept coming unglued.

One day, as he came into my office, I noticed that he was wearing a camouflage hat. I asked him if he was a real hunter, or if the cap was just for show. His immediate response made it clear to me. He was a legit woodsman, had been one all his life.

So I asked him about "buck fever."

The young man did a double take. "You know about buck fever?"

"Of course," I said. "But pretend I don't. Tell me about the first time you ever felt it."

He jumped right into the story. He'd been on hunting trips with his father before, but on *this* particular trip, he was finally going to be the one who took the shot. His big debut in the forest. I'm listening to this kid tell the story, the two of us in my office, but for him, he was right back in those woods. I could see it on his face.

He described every moment. His father tracking the buck. Lining up the shot for him. Everything was perfect. Time slowed down in a way that every hunter—and every athlete—knows.

He raised the rifle slowly, and looked down the barrel. Took a breath. But his heart was pounding in his chest.

Buck fever.

Pounding so loud, he was sure his father could hear it. Even his prey could hear it from fifty yards away.

Buck fever.

His palms were sweating. His eyes watered and his throat tightened. He couldn't breathe.

Take the shot! Why can't I take the shot! He's going to get away!

Buck fever!

Then: his father's voice, telling him to relax, to go through his routine, just as he'd practiced. Telling him to trust himself.

And then finally: a single shot rings out in the forest.

When the young pitcher came back from his reverie, I knew he'd found his own way to make a breakthrough.

Buck fever. For him, that was the key.

Everything that happened to him that day in the forest was normal, was *predictable*, and ultimately something he could manage and overcome. Pitching in a Division I baseball game may not be the same, but it shares some important similarities. He knew that he would have many emotions racing through his mind at once. Excitement, determination, but also raw fear. He could *predict*, without any doubt about it, that the fear would be there. It would *always* be there, waiting for him, every time he got up on that mound. It would never, ever go away.

So he normalized the concept of fear and began to see it as part of being human. He created the trigger words to control his own breathing and to ignite his focus.

He expected the fear. He accepted it. He *welcomed* it.

And then he would lean in, get the sign from his catcher, and throw that first strike.

What are some of your fears?

- fear of failure
- fear of abandonment
- fear of the unknown
- fear of another person
- fear of rejection
- fear of conflict
- fear of . . .

Honestly look at your own life and fill in this blank. What fears are sabotaging your potential, keeping you from fulfilling your hopes and dreams?

The lesson here is that fear—as well as anxiety, which is just another form of fear, the shadowy fear of what *might* happen—is as predictable as buck fever was for my young pitcher.

It is predictable, therefore manageable.

We can all expect to be fearful, anxious, nervous, apprehensive at times. Instead of trying to live in a world with no fear, try *embracing* fear. Turn it into a positive. Into a *passion*.

We love horror movies and roller coasters because of the rush and the exhilaration. Treat fear the same way: just a normal part of being human.

Think of the last time you took a big risk to make something happen. Do you remember that feeling? Most of the things in this life that make us truly excited, that challenge us physically, mentally, and spiritually . . .

The things that give us the best sense of accomplishment . . .

The things that make life worth living . . .

Those are the things that had us ready to crap our pants right before we did them. Am I right or am I wrong?

I'm not telling you to stop being afraid. I'm telling you to stop being afraid of being afraid.

Practice, train, and *rehearse* accepting fear and riding it like the wild stallion it is. As someone once said, "Ain't never been a horse that couldn't be rode. Ain't never been a rider couldn't be throwed." This stallion is waiting to be conquered, but he'll serve only a courageous rider. And if you do get thrown, just get your butt right back up in the saddle.

Courage is not the absence of fear.

Facing your fears. That's real courage.

STOP
BEING
AFRAID
OF BEING
AFRAID

—GREG HARDEN

CHAPTER 26

EXPOSE YOUR VAMPIRES TO THE LIGHT

In 1992, I was a guest speaker at Eastern Michigan University, for a summer bridge program to help struggling students improve their grades. One of those students was a young freshman named Lyonel Milton.

Lyonel was from Flint, one of the toughest cities in Michigan. In January of that year, his big brother had been killed. Now here was Lyonel, the first in his family to go to college, and all he could think about was his brother, who never got that same chance. As he told me later, he felt like he had to keep on living for both of them. He carried this burden with him every hour of every day. And that burden made his life a struggle.

But I didn't know that about Lyonel yet. All I saw was an angry young man. So I challenged him, along with the rest of the class, to think about his own *self-defeating attitudes and behaviors*. It's a theme I use often when I'm speaking to athletes, to businesspeople, to *anyone*. I talk more about this important topic in "Chapter 7: The Demon on Your Left Shoulder: Self-Defeating Attitudes and Behaviors," but I was essentially just asking Lyonel to think not about any external forces but rather about the things *inside* him that were holding him back.

I stayed in touch with Lyonel. It was two years later, at a workshop in my home, when I think I finally got through to him. This workshop was supposed to be a retreat for men, to talk about the things men usually can't or won't talk about: how to heal, how to forgive, how to work better together. But by the end of the meeting, Lyonel got into a heated argument with the group's leader.

I took Lyonel aside. "What the hell's going on?" I asked him. "Have I just been wasting my time with you?"

He started talking about losing his brother. Again. Not the first time I'd heard it, but this time I stopped him cold.

"Let him go," I said.

He looked at me like I'd just slapped him in the face.

"You're not going to bring him back," I said. "Let your brother rest in peace. It would break his heart if he knew you were using him as an excuse for why you're so angry and negative."

I think he finally realized in that moment that he'd never really accepted his brother's death. He was still reliving it every day. He wasn't moving on and living his own life.

"You're still angry about your brother. It's your unresolved issue, and it's one of the reasons why you have to act so *hard* all the time."

Lyonel had to believe that accepting his brother's death, embracing life, and moving forward did not mean he was abandoning his brother or loving him any less.

He would go on to become the director of student affairs for the School of Education at the University of Michigan. He's also an associate minister for the Bethel African Methodist Episcopal Church. We've been friends ever since, and like any of us, Lyonel is still a work in progress.

I talked to him just the other day, in fact. He'd had an outburst at work, and he called me. "You are forty years old and you still trust anger," I said. "But you're going to be all right."

What's your psychic vampire?

Think about it. Is it something in your past that may be crippling you, preventing you from seizing your confidence, your courage, your consistency?

Maybe it's a person, or a group of people.

Maybe it's an old wound. A bad decision. A grudge you want to hold on to forever.

You can't talk about it with anyone—let alone with yourself. You can't see it from a new perspective, one that would start draining your vampire of its power.

But that's the only way.

If you really want to make a breakthrough and become the person you've always dreamed of becoming, you have to find a way to expose your psychic vampires to the light. That's the only way to destroy them. The only way to break their hold over your mind, body, and spirit.

Talk to someone qualified if you have to, to help you let go of yesterday's baggage. To grieve, to recalibrate, to change your way of thinking.

In the fictional world of vampires, you know that they thrive in the darkness. If you keep them locked up in the closet, I guarantee you they'll be in there doing push-ups, sit-ups, getting stronger every single day. Believe me, you don't want to open up that door and get trapped inside when those vampires have built themselves up with two full cycles of strength training.

So be brave enough to look into your own darkness. Find your psychic vampires and drag them out into the healing light.

ANN WELCH BRAUN

TESTIMONIAL

Ann Welch Braun's personal transformation began when she met Greg just six months into her sobriety, as a new university student at the age of twenty-five. Ann was seeking extra support through a program in the hospital where Greg was working as a substance abuse counselor. With Greg's help, Ann went on to earn a master's degree with honors, then embarked on a thirteen-year career in educational sales with a subsidiary of Berkshire Hathaway. In 2001, Ann was hired by the University of Michigan's Medical Development Office to raise money for a new children's hospital—the Champions for Children Campaign. Based on her success in this effort, Ann was recruited to the University of Florida, where she served as associate dean of development and alumni affairs, and where she led a team of fundraising professionals that increased giving from $5 million to $60 million annually. She has also served as senior associate dean at the University of Southern California. Ann's twenty-year fundraising career has resulted in nearly $1 billion in private support for nonprofits.

"Despair is the great absurdity."

In 1982, I met Greg while seeking support in my sobriety. Sober for only six months, and beginning a college career at age twenty-five, I found that our weekly one-on-one sessions greatly increased my ability to focus on school, work, and sobriety, all at the same time. My constant angst of "impending doom" began to diminish as I put into practice Greg's powerful tools for building up my own narrative about who I was in the world. I came to understand that although I grew up in a loving home with dedicated parents and twelve siblings, I suffered from a culture of deep shame, leading to debilitating self-doubt.

I distinctly remember practicing one of Greg's early exercises to overcome my self-inflicted pain. I deliberately began listing and emphasizing all of my strengths, my skills, and my accomplishments. I practiced building up my own self-esteem, which was highly susceptible to all criticisms, real or imagined. Greg constantly reminded me that my mind needed to be my *ally* and not my enemy—a condition that was making my life so much harder than it needed to be.

As my anxiety subsided, I found this freed an unlimited amount of energy to focus on my school, work, and personal development. You could even say I was thriving for the first time in my life. By refocusing my previously squandered energy, I was growing into a healthier, more mature person capable of accomplishing so much more than ever before.

Many of the skills I developed over those three years working with Greg helped me build a better life. Based on Greg's coaching, I began to shape my own "personal philosophy," which still to this day guides my actions. I began to identify critical aspects of my values, my perspectives, and my goals—and how they guided my choices. This new philosophy replaced the shame-based perspectives that were inherited, unexamined, and yet highly impactful in my life. I also had a new understanding of a God who was far more loving, nonjudgmental, and empowering than the one I thought I had known in my youth.

The most important lesson Greg taught me was to focus on creating a future that was truly exciting, rather than reliving my past traumas and failures over and over again. A future in which I could be happy, healthy, and still a little crazy—but in a productive and deliberate manner.

As I continued to feel healthier, I entered the most highly productive years of my life, so different from the years of struggle and suffering that preceded my sobriety. Once I identified and dealt with the destructive behaviors of my youth, I realized that they had been robbing me of any sense of peace, joy, or enthusiasm.

I began to build momentum in life through successes at school, as reflected in scholarships, academic awards, and high grades. After graduating cum laude, I remained an active learner, turning my car into a library and eventually owning hundreds of educational recordings that continued to expand my awareness, my skills, and my self-esteem.

Another important thing Greg taught me was to realize that *despair is the great absurdity*. It would come to me whenever I felt trapped, without any options. Greg reinforced the deep belief within myself that there would always be options, if I looked carefully enough. He helped me to become more accepting of my unique qualities. This freed me to begin living into my own power, which led to leadership positions throughout my career. I literally went from those sessions with Greg in a basement office in Ypsilanti, Michigan, to a boardroom in Los Angeles, comfortably presenting to a group of billionaires.

Recently faced with a tragic loss, I was able to navigate my way to solid ground with Greg's voice echoing in my head. We always have a choice— whether we choose the negative self-talk that comes to us so easily, or whether we deliberately cultivate a positive and empowering perspective.

I was so lucky to cross paths with Greg Harden, who cared enough to help me build a foundation for a productive and impactful life and career. Almost forty years later, I am still living his lessons.

CHAPTER 27

. . . BY ITS COVER

I want you to picture a lecture room in a large hospital. Metal folding chairs all facing a whiteboard. Fluorescent lights buzzing overhead. You can smell the antiseptic in the air and hear the medical codes broadcast over the loudspeaker every few minutes. Now picture two dozen men sitting in those chairs. Almost every man is white, working class, age forty to fifty. Most come from families transplanted from Appalachia or from the Deep South.

None of them want to be here.

This is a thirteen-week lecture series, part of an outpatient rehab program administered by the treatment center in this hospital. If you're one of the attendees, there's a good chance that one of three people in your life have forced you to be here: your employer, your wife, or "a nudge from the judge."

Now picture me through the eyes of these men: the authority figure who's going to be lecturing these good ol' boys on the psychological and social impact of alcohol and drug use, every week for a solid hour and a half, for thirteen weeks. I think it's safe to say that many of these gentlemen had never had to sit still and listen to a fast-talking, social-working, obnoxiously optimistic Black man for more than a minute—unless it was mandated.

The first few lectures were tough, I'm not going to lie. I could *feel* the waves of anger and resentment from the men in this room. But I kept showing up every week, and instead of just giving them a ninety-minute didactic lecture, I tried to turn the whole experience into a group learning activity. I talked *to* them instead of *at* them. I challenged these men to share their own stories, to engage with each other and to *teach each other* how to change their lives.

I worked hard to build the program into something that could have a real effect on these men, and by the second year, some of the patients actually started bringing their families and friends to the lectures. A few of them even brought their drinking buddies. I admit, I started to feel comfortable, like I was getting pretty damned good at this. Like I could stand up in front of *anybody*, no matter where they came from or what they'd been through, and win them over. And then help them look at the reasons why they were here in this program, and how to use the help we offered.

Yeah, I thought I had this down.

Until the night *he* showed up.

I've been around enough offensive linemen and power forwards to know pretty much exactly how big this man was. So I'm going with six foot seven, 290 pounds. His thighs were the size of my torso. Reddish-blond hair, a beard with hints of gray. Camo and hunting boots. Simply the biggest, meanest hillbilly I'd ever seen in real life.

He sat down right in the front row. Stared a hole right through me as I cleared my throat, making it crystal clear that he was not happy about me, about this program, about being forced to be here, or about pretty much anything else that would happen in this room.

Now, I've been around some pretty tough characters in my life. On the streets, and for damned sure ever since I started working with alcoholics and addicts for a living. But this old boy . . . I knew I had my work cut out for me.

I gave him a couple of weeks to get comfortable before I finally decided it was time to reel him in. Get him participating in my group dynamic, just like every other hard case who ever walked through that door.

I asked him a question.

I got back nothing.

Just stone-cold silence.

Okay, I thought. *I don't give up that easy.* I came back to him, again and again, using every technique I knew to engage him. Eight weeks went by. And every attempt I made to connect with this mountain of a man came up empty. He just kept sitting there in the front row—*why did it always have to be the front row?*—and staring at me with those cold eyes, without ever saying a damned word.

I've got a vivid enough imagination, so I filled in the silence and started building my own picture of what was going on inside this hillbilly's head: he was a devout racist. A redneck hatemonger. He was just putting in his time here, going home and laughing about me at his KKK meetings. I knew it.

Then came Week Eleven. I'd been counting it down. Two more and I'd never have to see him sitting in that chair again, silently staring at me.

As the classroom filled up, I watched him come through the doorway. But instead of going to his seat, he came over to my desk. He towered over me, looking down and blocking out most of the light like a solar eclipse.

"I want to talk to you after class," he said with a Deep Southern drawl.

I nodded, not exactly sure how else to respond. *You'll have to catch me first* came to mind, but I didn't say it.

He went over to his usual seat in the front row, sat down, and proceeded to stare at me as usual while I began to conduct the class.

I had an hour and a half. I've never felt ninety minutes slip by so quickly.

When class was over, he stayed in his chair while everyone else left. Finally, we were alone in the classroom.

He stood up and approached my desk again. All the thoughts that had run through my mind about this man for eleven weeks straight—they all went right out the window, replaced by something else:

Pure fear and anxiety.

This is what he's been waiting for, I thought as I focused half my attention on the door—seemingly a mile away—and the other half on not pissing my pants. *He's going to break my skinny black neck like a twig.*

He opened his mouth and spoke:

"I just want you to know . . . I think you're a helluva man. I've learned more in these classes from you than I ever expected. I want to thank you for what you done for me."

Then he reached out with a hand the size of a baseball glove, took my hand in an almost-but-not-quite-bone-crushing grip, and shook it.

I was beyond flabbergasted. See, here was this man who I had already made up my mind about from the first second I saw him. I'd already decided, based solely on his outward appearance, that he *must* hate me and everyone else who looked like me.

It was so easy to see this man as my own post-slavery nightmare come to life. But I wasn't just wrong about him, I was almost *tragically* wrong. Because if two more weeks had passed without him saying anything, he would have been gone forever and I would have missed out on this opportunity to connect with him. Simply because of my own prejudice—that's right, *my* own prejudice—a word that is exactly the sum of its two parts: "pre-" and "judgment."

It's an experience that has stayed with me and has influenced me in ways that this man in my classroom never could have imagined.

Never judge a book by its cover. We've all heard that line a million times. It's a worn-out cliché, right? But think about what it really means.

Think about your own beliefs. Review the "absolutes" in your own mind and examine where they came from. Sometimes it may have been somebody else who told you at some point in your life that all Black men are criminals, or every big Southern white man wearing hunting camo and a John Deere hat must be a racist redneck.

Or every *whoever* must be *whatever*. Fill in your own blanks. Really think about it.

But remember this: Whenever you hear the word *all* or *every* come out of somebody's mouth, pay close attention. That person is about to say something extremely deep . . .

Or extremely stupid.

CHAPTER 28

THE TEAM, THE TEAM, THE TEAM

Of all the athletes I've worked with, swimmers are a breed apart.

It's a solitary sport like no other. Sure, runners run on their own, but they do it on a track or a road or a cross-country field, usually surrounded by other runners. A swimmer's life starts at dawn every day and takes place underwater, where even the *sounds* of the outside world are muffled into a distant hum. They spend countless hours in this world, endlessly going back and forth, staring at a line marked on the bottom of the pool. Collect a bunch of these solitary athletes together and you have a swim team. And it can get interesting.

One of the most "interesting" of all was a certain women's swim team a few years back. The entire team lived in three different houses on campus, which is not unusual. But when all of the hard partyers happen to live in one house, and all of the straight arrows live in another, and everyone living in the third house is stuck in the middle . . . let's just say it was not a good dynamic.

The team was really struggling that year. Where there should have been unity and encouragement, there was only division and anger. The captain was a young woman named Jen Arndt. She may not have been the strongest swimmer on the team, but she gave everything to the team. She gave 100 percent, 100 percent of the time, in the pool and on dry land. She was the one person trying the hardest to bring the team together, but one of the biggest problems she had to deal with was the rampant violation of team rules, especially when it came to alcohol. She and her two cocaptains had laid it all out clearly at the beginning of the season. No drinking during the forty-eight hours before a competition. Anyone breaking that rule gets a talk from a friend, then a captain, then from two or three captains, then a whole group intervention. And then, finally, it goes to the coaching staff.

It didn't take long to get to the coaching staff, which is where everything started to fall apart. That's where I came in. I met with the captains, and they asked for my help—which meant getting up at 5:00 a.m. every Saturday to meet with the captains at 6:00 a.m., right before practice.

The first thing we had to do was to get the coaches on board. The captains needed more support from them. They needed their sanction to hold the rest of the team accountable and to demand higher standards both in and out of the water.

Once they had that, they went back to the whole team.

It was late in the season, with the conference championships right around the corner. The entire team was gathered together for a no-holds-barred meeting. Everything on the table. Nothing held back. Brutal honesty.

Now, I couldn't just stand up in front of them as an authority figure in that meeting. As bad as things were, I had to trust in the team dynamic. I had to pose the right questions, plant the right seeds, and trust that somebody was going to stand up and say the right thing at just the right time. Something that would finally make everyone in the room face the issues that were tearing this team apart.

To finally come together, as a team, while there was still time to do it.

And it happened. I watched the team, led by the captain, Jen Arndt (who would go on to become a great swim coach, no surprise), begin to heal that day as they became honest and open with themselves and with their coaches—and as the coaches trusted the process, opened up, and showed vulnerability and a willingness to learn from their swimmers.

Did you ever see Al Pacino's speech in *Any Given Sunday*? It was just as good as that moment.

Either we heal now, as a team . . .

Or we will die as individuals.

Or better yet, I know I quoted Bo Schembechler once before, but I have to do it one more time:

No man is more important than The Team.

No coach is more important than The Team.

The Team, The Team, The Team.

And if we think that way, all of us, everything that you do, you take into consideration, what effect does it have on my Team?

I could *feel* the change in the air. It was real; it was tangible. Did every single swimmer buy into it? Maybe not. But those "haters" had now become the minority. They no longer had any influence on the rest of the team.

Their self-defeating attitudes and behaviors were held in check by the rest of the team.

As the team "shaved and tapered" for the conference championships, the team's numbers indicated that they would almost certainly finish in sixth place—fifth if they were lucky. These are the hard numbers that rule swimming, and they're hardly ever wrong. There are no referees to blame for a bad result, not in this sport. You can't blame your teammates for not passing the ball to you, or the goalie for letting in a bad goal. In swimming, the clock is the only judge, and the clock never lies.

I was in the stands for every race in that conference championship, and if this were a movie . . . well, you know what that result would be. A stunning come-from-nowhere victory, right?

That didn't happen.

But what I saw was something just as good, maybe even better. The team that should have finished sixth came in second in the conference. And when the final results were announced, the team leapt to their feet, screamed and danced and laughed as if they had just won the national championship. They were more excited than the team that actually came in first, because they finally came together and did it as a team.

I'll never forget that moment. Or that team.

Remember "Give 100 percent, 100 percent of the time?" When you can create that mindset within a team dynamic, it doesn't even matter anymore if you win, lose, or draw. This "win, lose, or draw" attitude can give your team a new and complete sense of freedom. You're going to give 100 percent, you're going to fight all the way to the end, and you'll be able to live with any outcome.

If you win, you will be grateful, but you will never take it for granted.

If you lose, you will know that you gave everything you had. Your self-worth and your self-esteem will remain intact.

That's the ultimate goal. To be so invested, so committed, and so determined that *even in defeat*, everyone with you and around you will be in awe, and even your opponent will wish you were on their team.

ERIK CAMPBELL

TESTIMONIAL

Erik "Soup" Campbell played football for Michigan from 1984 to 1987, one of the few players to start as a true freshman for Bo Schembechler. Since graduating, he has coached at several NCAA programs (including Michigan) as well as in the Canadian Football League. He is currently the passing game coordinator and wide receivers coach at Bowling Green State University.

**"For the first time in your life,
you're a member of a team, above anything else."**

I was on the first football team that Greg Harden talked to. I'll never forget meeting him, sitting down and talking with him. One thing you knew right away, he was a guy who was able to get your attention by bringing the message that we could relate to.

What he did was, he opened your eyes up as a young man, about *life* and about seeing things in a whole new way. Certain things in your behavior, why you do things a certain way and what the consequences are.

He really helped us understand the feelings behind what we were doing, our motivations, our "why's." He told us what we'd be going through, as players, as students, and as men. And later, I'd look back and say, "How did you know that?" It was amazing how he knew the struggles that we would all go through.

Even today, I still carry the lessons he taught me. Understanding your own mindset and your own behaviors and where they come from.

One of the most important things he taught us was how to become a real member of a team. In high school we were all the all-state or the all-this or that, but now those days were over and we were part of a team above anything else, maybe for the first time in our lives.

Remember, we played for Bo Schembechler. Talk about being a part of a *team*.

I've been part of teams ever since then, for over thirty years as a coach, and I still use the lessons Greg taught me. They're all a part of me now, and I try to share those lessons with all of the young men that come through our program. It's a step-by-step process as they go through life, and I teach them the same things that Greg taught me.

To believe in yourself.

To believe in each other and in the team.

To be more than a football player.

To become a man of character and substance.

That's why I'm still in coaching. What Greg gave to me, I can now pass on to others. And then they go out into the world and keep paying it forward.

CHAPTER 29

ONE MORE TEAM . . .
AND THE ULTIMATE CHALLENGE

It was May 2018. I was standing at the podium in a large conference room in San Diego, California. Facing me were seasoned professionals from the medical technology industry, brought together here from all four corners of the world.

When I say four corners, I mean it. There were four separate companies represented here, from different parts of the world:

North America.

The United Kingdom.

Australia.

Saudi Arabia.

Four very different groups, from four very different cultures, that even now had segregated themselves into four separate quadrants of the conference room.

On paper, these four groups were now parts of a single entity, brought together in this room to form the largest multinational corporation the industry had ever seen. But "on paper" doesn't make a team.

The first stranger was introduced and stood up to address the room. He was the new CEO of this company. He didn't come from one of the four subgroups. He was the outsider brought in to somehow make this huge merger work. And not just work but *thrive* in a highly competitive market. To be the most successful medical technology corporation in the world.

He spoke for an hour and twenty minutes. He was serious. He was impressive. Everyone in the room listened to him carefully, because he was now the most important person in their lives.

When he sat down, it was time for the second unfamiliar face to speak. That was me.

I stood up and looked over the faces in the room. I saw curiosity. I saw anxiety. I saw doubt and concern. I saw four separate groups that had come a long way, brought here together and told that they were now a team.

But I didn't see a team.

That's why I was here. To help the four different groups in this room begin the quest to become a team.

And I had one afternoon to do it.

It's no accident that this chapter comes right after "Chapter 28: The Team, The Team, The Team." In that case, I was trying to help a dysfunctional swim team, made up of individuals with very different personalities, finally come together and create a real team. The challenge was daunting, but it wasn't the first time I had seen a group of athletes fail to come together and create something more meaningful, and more powerful, than just a team photo to hang on the wall.

Every year, around 950 athletes come to the University of Michigan campus. About 250 of them are here for the first time. Their whole lives, no matter what the sport, they've been doing nothing but playing for themselves. Everyone else is just a competitor, maybe a teammate wearing the same uniform for a season or two, but in the end just another athlete focused on his or her own future.

When these athletes get to our campus, the future is *now*. And some, for the first time in their lives, have to learn how to become part of a team.

Some have come from small towns, some from inner cities, some from other countries entirely. Different backgrounds, different cultures, different experiences. Each one of these athletes has to make a huge adjustment, not just athletically, but also academically and socially. There are new rules all around them. New expectations. New demands.

It's a sad fact of life that some of these athletes just aren't ready for these big changes. And just as sadly, it's a fact of life that some athletic teams never become teams at all.

Fortunately, the swim team in the previous chapter did find a way to come together as a team, and the result was a totally unexpected second-place finish in the Big Ten championship meet. Those are the stakes we usually talk about when we talk about sports teams: wins and losses, placements in conferences, and national championships.

But fast-forward a few years to this day in San Diego, in a conference room filled with medical technology professionals from four different companies around the globe. The stakes today were the careers of every person in that room, and the future of their families. The stakes were the success or failure of a multinational corporation.

And because of what this corporation was trying to do—creating new and better ways to ensure quality control in medical facilities, reducing the chances of errors and miscommunications that could put vulnerable patients at risk—the stakes were even higher: literally saving lives.

"Everyone in this room is facing extreme change right now," I said to them. "You've got a new boss, a whole new organization. You're putting together people from different cultures, different backgrounds. None of you have ever done anything like this before. So no matter how old or how young you are, which part of the world you come from, the fear and the self-doubt are going to show up in this room."

I looked down at all of the faces. The fear and the self-doubt had already arrived.

"The fear and self-doubt are predictable," I said, repeating the line I've said to thousands of people in every conceivable circumstance. "Therefore, they are *manageable*. You have to *anticipate* the fear. *Anticipate* the self-doubt. And then *deliberately and intentionally* decide if you're going to allow yourself to be consumed by it."

I took a moment to let that sink in. To let each person in the room begin to formulate his or her own decision.

"I've studied your products," I said. "I see what you're trying to do. Make hospitals safer. Make medicine work better. You're trying to *save lives*."

I saw a few people nodding their heads.

"All you have to do now," I said, "is get out of your own heads, rise above the stereotypes you may have about each other. About what it means to come from these other places. North America. The United Kingdom. Australia. Saudi Arabia. I want everyone in this room to decide right now that they're going to focus on the core mission that you all share. Because the languages may be different, the cultures may be different, *but the goal is the same.* In the end, you all have more in common than you realize!"

That was actually just the first of two meetings that day. In the next session, having helped everyone in the room understand the challenges they faced as a team trying to come together, I broke it down and tried to talk to everyone as individuals.

Because ultimately, being a great team member starts with believing in yourself. Being committed to becoming the person that you can be—in other words, everything else that I've been talking about in this book. Becoming the world's greatest expert on yourself, identifying your own self-defeating attitudes and behaviors, controlling the controllables. Commit, improve, maintain. That was the second part of my message, because at this particular time in the history of this company, there was a desperate need for every single person in the room to go to the next level in his or her personal excellence.

I got a nice note from the president a few days later, telling me that I had "genuinely connected with everyone's heart and soul." It's not quite the same as a football team giving you a game ball, or getting soaked at the edge of a swimming pool. But I was just as grateful for the kind words.

I know there will be many other teams, both athletic and professional, that I'll have the privilege of addressing. But no matter what kind of team, how big or small, how minor or major their problems may be, I'll always bring with me the one core message that Bo Schembechler said better than anyone:

Nobody is more important than The Team.

The Team.

The Team.

The Team.

WALEED SAMAHA

Waleed Samaha has known Greg Harden ever since meeting him as a high school student. He worked for many years as an educator, social worker, and basketball coach. After fourteen seasons coaching the boys' basketball team at Ann Arbor Huron High School, Waleed left to become Michigan Basketball's Director of Operations. After one season at the college level, his heart led him back to Ann Arbor Huron, where he is now a general education social worker and is also coaching the girls' basketball team.

**"Greg was doing cognitive behavioral
therapy before they even called it that."**

I was friends with Glenn "Shemy" Schembechler (Bo's son) when I was just a kid, and that's when I met Greg Harden. Bo had hired Greg to talk to his kids, and I happened to be there when he was giving his presentation to the players. And I was like, *Oh my God, that's the most awesome thing I've ever seen.* It was my senior year of high school, and I told him, "I don't even know what you do for a living, but whatever that is you just did, I want to do that someday."

When he found out I wasn't even in college yet, he told me, "When you graduate, come back and see me." So literally the day after I got my undergraduate degree, I walked into his office and I said, "I'm back!"

I hounded him for days, and whether I just wore him down or he thought, okay, maybe this kid is crazy enough to do this—either way, he agreed to take me on as an intern.

When you were with Greg Harden, it would never be about him. That was the best thing about him. You'd be with him for an hour and he would disarm you and you would be willing to say whatever you needed to say. Because he was a great listener. Probably his greatest skill is listening.

Listening is a lost art! But Greg is a master.

He became my life coach, my mentor, my friend. Outside of my father, Greg is the single most influential person in my life.

I apply the lessons I've learned from Greg in every area of my life. As a husband, as a father, as an educator, as a coach. I find myself asking myself, "What would G say right now?"

Probably one of the greatest lessons I learned from Greg, as a coach, was that you need to show the face that your kids need to see, right now. Sometimes you got to get in their backsides, sometimes you just have to be aware of the emotion that they're feeling, and you have to show the face that's going to pull them out of that emotion. If it's a self-defeating mindset or attitude, you can't go in there screaming and hollering and raising hell, because that's not what they need right now. They need a confidence boost. They need to rechannel that energy.

As a coach, as a leader, as a father, in business, in family, any time you're leading people, you need to listen to what they need. Greg's leadership style is all about empowering people, about getting people to believe in themselves. Because sometimes you have to believe in people before they can believe in themselves. When you build up their confidence and their skills, you create this mindset of excellence.

I remember when he was talking to Charles Woodson, and Greg told him, "If you allow yourself to be defined as just a football player, we have failed you." This is a Heisman Trophy winner, and he's telling him he's a student first, not a football player.

Now, as I've become more experienced in my field as an educator, I've been drawn to cognitive behavioral therapy (CBT), which is basically training people to think differently. Because the best way to feel differently and to behave differently is to start with *thinking* differently. Greg was all about that before they even called it CBT. Replacing negative thoughts with positive, productive thoughts.

I use the same approach, not just with kids in school, but when I'm coaching other staff members or even with parents. When there's a problem to face, that's the first question I ask. We have control over how we're going to think about this. What are we going to choose?

Greg will often use humor to do this kind of work with you. He'll make you laugh at yourself. Make you see the way you're thinking and how it's not working. And why you have to get real with yourself.

At some point, you have to stop fooling yourself. And change the way you think!

A FEW WORDS FROM GREG ON WALEED SAMAHA

Waleed Samaha may not be a household name, known by all, but if there was ever an individual who embraced and trained himself to take these lessons and own them, teach them, and promote them, he is that guy.

And if there was ever an individual who made me believe in my own strategies and techniques, it was Waleed. My trust and confidence in him, and the way he took this work to the next level, is unwavering.

Thank you, Waleed, for your faith, loyalty, and friendship.

CHAPTER 30

SAY THANK YOU
(AND THEN SHUT YOUR MOUTH)

Sarah Kamstra was a diver at Michigan, a key member of the team that would win the 2016 Big Ten Championship. She was a Division I finalist on the 3-meter board and platform and was named an All-American by the National Strength and Conditioning Association, and a Scholar All-American by the College Swimming and Diving Coaches Association of America.

Smart.

Strong.

By any measure, a success, right?

Remember the young woman from "Chapter 18: SWOT Yourself," who had the dream life but couldn't stop the negative self-talk in her head? What is it that makes so many of us simply and utterly unable to accept that we might actually be good at something?

Why can't we just accept a compliment, say THANK YOU, and then shut up?

I challenged Sarah with this idea, because, to quote the exact words she's given me permission to use: "I lacked confidence in who I was as an individual. I would justify even the smallest of compliments and ramble on about things that had nothing to do with the compliment, just to get the spotlight off of me."

I asked her to practice the art of saying THANK YOU and then shutting up. It may sound simple, but try it sometime!

"Over the next few weeks," Sarah said, "I struggled. I constantly caught myself justifying my behaviors rather than accepting the compliments and the sincerity that often came from those interactions. The more often I found myself justifying the compliment, the more irritated I began to get. There were times that I would literally say thank you and bite my tongue."

But after several weeks of practice, her confidence finally started to bloom. "I was able to accept the moments and appreciate the interactions. I learned to love myself more than I had previously, and by loving myself more, accepting the compliments through the two words of 'thank you' got easier. By being aware of that self-defeating behavior, I opened a whole new wave of self-growth and acceptance. So now, whenever I receive a compliment, I say 'thank you' and then proceed to shut up."

How many times have you done exactly the same thing yourself? Somebody compliments you and you immediately discount their attempt to acknowledge something positive about you?

You correct them by explaining the facts. "Oh, this dress/suit is old as dirt." Or you instantly compliment them to neutralize their statement. You are so uncomfortable that sometimes you just ignore the positive efforts completely as you change the subject.

You correct them, practically *fight* with them if you have to. Anything to avoid accepting that compliment. "Oh, this suit just *makes* me look thinner." "That project wasn't nearly as hard as it looked." "I'm really not as good at that as you think I am." You're literally trying to convince the person complimenting you that they shouldn't believe their own eyes. And then you change the subject immediately before they have the chance to argue with you.

I have worked with so many amazing people in my life—in athletics, in business, in a hundred other professions. Some were brilliant. Some were so attractive you'd literally have to call them breathtaking. Some were the most caring and compassionate people you could ever hope to meet in your entire life.

And still, to this day, I am amazed at the general human inability to accept a compliment. In fact, I've noticed that the better you are at giving compliments to others, the worse you are at accepting them for yourself. And hey, I'm not immune to this myself. I know I'm pretty good at building people up and lifting their spirits. It's what I try to do every single day. But I have to be aware of how uncomfortable I get whenever someone else tries to make me feel like I'm the special one.

I mean, on some level I get it. We're taught from an early age to be gracious and humble. Not to be boastful or arrogant. *Pride goeth before a fall.*

Or maybe it's simply a matter of learned behavior. A strategy you've developed to make sure that others don't put you up on a pedestal. Because you *know* what can happen next.

Whatever the reason, I want to ask you to stop automatically deflecting compliments. I know it's not easy. It took me a long time to train myself to just say THANK YOU and then to keep my mouth shut. What helped me was realizing that by accepting a compliment, I was honoring the person who gave it to me. Instead of automatically rejecting their perspective, I was essentially complimenting them right back, by letting them know that I recognized the value of what they were giving me.

Just as importantly, I realized that as a human being, I *need* compliments. We all do. Think about it. Think about those times when a well-timed compliment was exactly what you needed. You don't have to have somebody complimenting you every five minutes, but think about those important times in your life when you really *needed* the sense of reinforcement that comes with the gift of acknowledgment. To deny yourself the power of that gift is to deny yourself something as essential as food and water.

Especially if you're doing the work in the rest of this book. If you're practicing, training, and rehearsing giving 100 percent, 100 percent of the time. That's when a compliment can let you know that what you're doing is really working, and other people in your life can see it. Rejecting a compliment *then* is like rejecting the value of your work. Like rejecting your own self-value.

If you are passionate about pursuing "self-love and self-acceptance," you will receive heartfelt compliments with grace and humility.

So I'll say it one more time: The next time somebody compliments you . . .

Say THANK YOU.

And then shut your mouth.

CHAPTER 31

WHISPERS AND BRICKS

I haven't had many interns working directly for me, but we always have a number of them working elsewhere in the athletic department. One of the best was a young man named Jackson Weber. He had given his best to us, and I was sorry to see him leave. Jackson was not just as sad as I was; he was devastated.

His internship was ending, his money was running out, his lease was up, and he had no idea where he'd be living next. There was some trouble with his family back home, and Jackson felt the weight of responsibility to help—but he had big dreams that didn't include moving back into his parents' house.

He had come so far already. His upbringing hadn't been easy. Most people looked at him and saw a handsome, fit, polished, articulate young man—someone who was clearly on the road to success. But I knew that behind that facade was an overweight, lost child who had struggled for most of his life. But as far as Jackson had come, his future now felt uncertain to him. Leaving the university, where he had finally found his niche, was a true crossroads moment in his life.

I guarantee you this: I learn as much from the people I mentor as they ever do from me, and what I learned from Jackson as he faced his crossroads is something I'll never forget.

He told me about someone he'd met years ago, an old man who was living on the streets. That's the kind of man most other people would walk right by, maybe dropping a quarter into his cup but never really interacting with him. But Jackson engaged with this homeless man on multiple occasions and had real conversations. And this man said something to Jackson that would stay with him for the rest of his life:

"God speaks in whispers and bricks."

Think about that for a minute. Isn't it the truth?

How many times have you received a "whisper" in your life? You're on a certain path, you may even know in your gut that you need to change direction. But you keep going.

You can watch how a certain person treats the other people in his life, for instance, but you say to yourself, "Well, he/she/they haven't treated *me* that way yet." The key word is *yet*, because they're *showing* you, through their actions, what kind of person they are. The way they treat everyone else around them is demonstrating, in crystal-clear fashion, exactly what kind of person they are.

The whisper is sometimes subtle, but it is unmistakable. If we ignore the whisper, maybe we avoid a small amount of pain in the short term. But then what do we get?

A brick to the side of the head, which *always* brings a hell of a lot more pain. But sometimes that's what it takes. A clear and undeniable message to get your attention! An unmissable signal to get you to change your course, your actions, and possibly your attitudes and behaviors.

It was time for Jackson to move on, but his ability to reinvent himself, to read the handwriting on the wall, would lead him down a great path to a great life. He is an entrepreneur and husband now and is exceptional in everything he sets his mind to do.

But I'll always remember the lesson he left with me.

Increase your sensitivity to the whispers in your life. That angel on your right shoulder, who speaks to you in your quietest thoughts and your deepest dreams. Listen carefully, because that angel whispers the truth.

Don't wait for the brick, because a brick always hurts a lot more.

CHAPTER 32

FACING THE CHALLENGE OF PUBLIC SPEAKING

What if I told you, you're going to stand up in front of five hundred people tomorrow, and you're going to speak to them for twenty minutes?

What are you feeling right now?

Are you sweating? Are your hands shaking? Do you have to change your pants?

The fancy Latin term for fear of public speaking is *glossophobia*, and I read somewhere that three out of four people suffer from it. So you're not alone! But at some point in your life, you're probably going to have to face it. And I have some concrete ideas to make it a lot easier.

Leah Robertson, a water polo player at Michigan, had maybe the worst case of glossophobia I've ever seen. She was tall, attractive, and athletic, mind you—one of the best players on the team and an all-around fantastic person. But the thought of standing up in front of an audience at the end of the season was giving her nightmares.

The first thing I told her was that she needed to *expect* the demons of fear and self-doubt to show up that night. She wouldn't be human if they didn't.

And because those demons are *predictable*, they are therefore *manageable*. (I think you've probably heard me say this before.)

"Expect them," I said, "and in fact, *embrace* them. Shake their hands, tell them they're a little late, tell them you don't have time for them now. They can have a seat and you'll be back with them when you're done."

Because, of course, that's what real courage is. Not the *absence* of fear, but proceeding with your business *despite* fear ("Chapter 25: Fear, Courage, and 'Buck Fever'").

Ultimately, the challenge really has nothing to do with the audience at all. There's probably nobody out there with a weapon to hurt you. In fact, every single person in that room *wants* you to do well. The challenge is completely inside your own head.

Which means what?

It's the one thing you can control.

CONTROL THE CONTROLLABLES.

If you need help doing that, here's the best tip I can give you: Make sure that you have the first two minutes of what you're going to say completely memorized, forward and backward. Own that first two minutes. Prepare it; learn it; practice it obsessively until it's a part of you. Until you can recite it standing on your head.

Now, when you begin, you'll have those first two minutes down cold. You'll be flying on autopilot for 120 seconds. And you'll see an amazing thing happen during that time:

You'll relax. You'll ease into yourself. You'll see that the people in the room are with you, not against you.

(And then the next time you get up to speak in front of a group of people, it'll get even easier!)

Leah Robertson got up in front of that audience at the end of the season and sailed through those first two minutes, and then kept going. She's a business owner now. She does public speaking all the time and never thinks twice about it.

Try this technique the next time you're faced with the same challenge, and I am confident you'll nail it!

CHAPTER 33

WHEN YOU'RE INTERVIEWING SOMEONE, LET THEM TELL YOU WHO THEY ARE

I've worked with many executives who hire people for their businesses every day, and I've interviewed more than a few applicants for positions in my roles as manager, supervisor, and director. The one thing I've learned about interviewing is actually a very simple concept:

Let them tell you who they are.

Maybe you've heard the old story about the man who owned a gas station in a small town. One day, a car pulls in to gas up and the driver gets out.

"We're just moving into town," the driver says. "What are the people like here?"

"Before I tell you," the gas station owner says, "why don't you tell me about the people from the town you're moving away from?"

"Nastiest people in the world," the driver says. "Not friendly, not considerate. Just awful, and I can't tell you how glad we are to get away from them."

"Well," the owner says, "I'm afraid you're going to find the same kind of people here."

Several hours later, a second car pulls in. The second driver gets out to pump the gas.

"We're just moving into town," the driver says. "What are the people like here?"

The owner repeats the same question he asked the first driver. "What were the people like in the town you're coming from?"

"They were wonderful," the driver says. "Just the nicest, friendliest people you could ever find. We're sorry to be leaving them."

"Well, you're in luck," the owner says. "We got the same kind of people here."

It's a simple story, but you get the point. I recommend using the same technique when you're interviewing someone for your company or organization. Ask them to describe the best experience they had at their former job or school, then their worst experience. Then ask about the best boss they ever had (or maybe the best teacher if they're just coming out of school), and then the worst.

Now, listen very carefully, because they're about to tell you everything you need to know about them.

Anyone can have a bad experience or a bad boss, but listen to how they describe that situation or person. Do they take any ownership or responsibility for whatever was negative? Can they see more than just their own narrow perspective?

It was a bad match. To be fair, I was not the right person at the right time. They needed someone with different skills.

Or is it just a parade of whining and complaining?

My boss was such an asshole. He was totally unreasonable about everything. I swear, I think I'm cursed, because I always end up working for people like this.

It's an extreme example, but you get the idea. Try to imagine how they'd talk about *you* someday if things didn't work out perfectly.

In a way, this is an extension of what I'm talking about in "Chapter 31: Whispers and Bricks," and it applies to a potential mate just as much as a potential hiree. The way someone treats the other people in their life will tell you what kind of person they are.

So when someone tells you who they are, in the interview room or anywhere else, listen!

I just want to add one more note here, because interviewing and hiring has been such a big part of my job in my thirty-four years at Michigan. Instead of just sitting on the other side of a desk and asking the same old questions, here are a few of the best interviewing techniques I've used instead: panel interviews, role-plays, small group discussions, behavioral interviews, and formal presentations.

In each of these formats, you're creating a more dynamic, real-life scenario, and you can discover a great deal more about your candidates. You can get a real sense of how they interact with other people and whether they might be a good fit for your organization and your existing culture—or the culture you're trying to create.

CHAPTER 34

WHEN YOU'RE BEING INTERVIEWED, TURN IT AROUND!

I can't talk about interviewing ("Chapter 33: When You're Interviewing Someone, Let Them Tell You Who They Are") without saying something about being on the other side of that table. We've all been there. I know it can be nerve-racking. But I've counseled more young people heading out into the job market than I can count, and here's what I always tell them:

First of all, be aware of everything I said in that last chapter about telling the interviewer who you are by the way you answer questions about your past experiences. If you come across as the person who's been cursed by a long string of asshole bosses, I guarantee you, you just lost the job—because the common denominator in all of your bad situations was *you*.

If you take ownership for bad experiences, if you have perspective about why your relationships with a past boss didn't work out, then you're going to be coming across in a whole different way (even if your last boss *was* an asshole).

Beyond that point, the second important thing to remember is that *it's your job in any interview to make sure the interviewer talks just as much as you do.*

That's right. You need to turn it around and interview the interviewer. Because that's exactly what this interview should be about. You're trying to find out if this place is the best use of your time and talent, just as much as they're trying to find out if you're the right person for the job.

You already know you're going to have a job *somewhere*. And you're going to do an amazing job, wherever you go. Now you're just deciding if this is the place where that's going to happen.

I'm not talking about being arrogant or cocky. You should leave your ego at the door when you walk in. But at the same time, you should know in your head and in your heart that *hiring you is the best thing they could ever do.*

In the end, it's *their* mission to convince *you* to work for *them*. Because it's not just them making a decision. It should always be just as much *your* decision, on where you're going to be spending so much of your time and energy.

And if you have this attitude, you'll actually increase your chances of getting hired. If you're asking them these questions, how can they not be impressed by how insightful you are and how committed you are to knowing exactly where you want to go? All of a sudden, they'll be trying to convince you to be a part of their company—and at that point, you pretty much have the job!

Think about this before your next interview. Practice, train, and rehearse having this mindset.

And then see what happens.

CHAPTER 35

IF YOU HAPPEN TO BE A GOLFER

... then may God have mercy on your soul. Also, keep reading.
If you don't golf, be thankful and skip this chapter.

I'll admit this up front: I grew up hating the game of golf. Some of the hate may have been based on class and race. Some of it was outright ignorance about the game—not knowing anything about it and not wanting to know anything about it, because in my mind it wasn't a real sport, anyway!

The ball's just sitting there on a tee. It's not moving. And I've got fourteen different clubs I can choose to take a big swing at it? Nobody's going to try to block my shot or defend against me in any way? In fact, they're going to keep real quiet so I can concentrate?

Nope, not a real sport. No, thank you.

So when the women's golf coach came into my office one day, asking if I could work with one of his players who was really struggling, I had a problem.

"Coach," I said, "I'm afraid I don't know anything about your sport. I mean, I can talk to her in general about being a student athlete, about being her best self . . ."

I didn't say anything about not liking his sport, or about not considering it a sport at all. I left that part out of the conversation.

In the end, he was fine with me giving his player the general pep talk. Now, I had a few days to get ready for it, and I figured to myself, this is a varsity sport at the University of Michigan and you're going to talk to one of the players for the first time, so maybe you should actually prepare for this by learning a little bit more about the game.

So yes, I actually got myself some clubs and I went out to the driving range.

I got a bucket of balls, teed one up, grabbed a driver, and lined up the face of the club behind the ball. The club felt good in my hands, and the way the ball was just sitting there . . .

With my muscle mass, I thought, *and with my athleticism, I'm going to hit this thing three hundred yards.*

I brought the club back and swung. The ball went maybe a hundred yards, well right of straight, like a foul ball down the first base line.

I teed up another ball. *Swing a little harder this time.*

This time, the ball went fifty yards instead of a hundred.

This is ridiculous.

A few worm-burners later, I was back in my car, driving home.

I still had an appointment with the golfer, so I went out and bought a couple of books. I studied them carefully, tried to find some common ground with the other sports I knew a lot better. By the time the young golfer was sitting in my office, I was still the world's most unqualified teacher on the game, but that hadn't stopped me from developing my own system:

The six T's.

Tempo and timing.

Technique and training.

Temperament and trust.

"The tempo and timing," I told her, "you know about those already. Everything in the swing working together. Smooth and relaxed. But those are the only things you should have in your mind while you're swinging the club. Tempo. Timing. That's it. Nothing else."

She nodded. So far, she was with me.

"Technique and training," I said. "Honing your skills. Continuous improvement." Here I was on familiar ground, at least, as I led her through my lessons on practicing, training, and rehearsing giving 100 percent, 100 percent of the time ("Chapter 11: The 100 Percent Challenge"), and continuous improvement ("Chapter 19: Commit, Improve, Maintain").

She was still with me, listening to every word I said.

"Finally," I said, "temperament and trust. We go from the physical to the mental. A belief system, increasing your confidence in who you are and what you're doing. Trusting you know how to play this game. Building yourself up instead of beating yourself up. Like Ben Hogan, who said that 'great mishits are the name of the game.' Or Tiger Woods, who was the total master of the mental game. Never let one shot affect the next. Bogey, birdie, eagle—it didn't matter. He let it go and moved on to the next." ("Chapter 22: The Value of a Short Memory.")

I sent her on her way, just hoping I had helped her a little.

The next time I saw her, she had become the second-best golfer on the team.

It's just a fluke, I thought. But the coach immediately sent me his captain to work with.

We went through the same ideas, the six T's: Tempo and timing. Technique and training. Temperament and trust.

Now I had two golfers playing lights out.

That's when it dawned on me: I hadn't approached the game this way myself! I had just assumed that I could step onto the driving range and muscle the ball anywhere I wanted it to go. And got frustrated and quit as soon as I saw that it didn't work that way.

So I made myself a promise. Instead of giving the game two weeks and expecting to be good at it, I'd give it two years, using the same principles I'd given to the Michigan golfers. I surrendered my ego, allowed myself to fail, to fail *badly*. I let myself enjoy the quest to get better, to have fun pursuing perfection in a game where perfection is impossible ("Chapter 21: It's Perfectly Okay Not to Be Perfect"). Most importantly, I deliberately and intentionally decided that I would be patient with myself, *laugh* at myself, and accepted that it would take two years of practice before I could even consider myself someone who understood the game.

Of course, you know what happened next. Within a year, I was hooked.

One of the most eye-opening experiences I've ever had, not just in golf but in any sport, was playing with the young woman who had been responsible for me trying to learn more about this game in the first place. She was five foot two, maybe 110 pounds. I thought I was stronger than ammonia, but I watched her outdrive me by thirty to forty yards on every tee.

Her swing looked nothing like mine! It was elegant; it was smooth. It had nothing to do with muscle power at all. It was all . . . yes, *tempo and timing*. I was still trying to learn my own lessons!

I've kept playing in the years since, and I've never even come close to breaking par. But that's okay. The game has taught me so much about myself and given me so much insight into the lessons I've been trying to pass along to young athletes.

Like Cooper Marody ("Chapter 17: Get Out of Your Own Way!"), I had to learn how to get out of my own way—because if there was ever a game that *demanded* that, it's golf.

I had to learn not to beat myself up after bad shots, because it was only when I stopped worrying about failure that I started to improve.

And finally, I had to learn maybe the hardest lesson of all: Golf is just a game, and it's supposed to be *fun*.

Of all the sports I've ever played, I think golf may be the best metaphor for life. It's one of the most mentally demanding of all sports. Golf trains you, better than anything, in how to deal with yourself, and it exposes every weakness if you don't. If you're not committed to becoming your best self, the game of golf will always be your enemy, never an ally.

And it won't be much fun!

THE SIX T'S OF GOLF:
TEMPO & TIMING
TECHNIQUE & TRAINING
TEMPERAMENT & TRUST

–GREG HARDEN

CHAPTER 36

PLEASE REMEMBER THESE SEVEN THINGS

I read in a psychology textbook that the human mind has just enough short-term memory to easily remember seven things, so as I near the close of this book, I'm going to give you exactly seven things to remember:

BECOME THE WORLD'S GREATEST EXPERT ON YOURSELF, so that you can become the very best version of yourself.

CONTROL THE CONTROLLABLES. Never forget that you are the only person who has control over your own mind—over your thoughts and ultimately over your feelings.

PRACTICE, TRAIN, AND REHEARSE giving 100 percent, 100 percent of the time. Because if you make this your mindset, then on your absolutely worst day, you're still going to be better than the average person on their best day.

COMMIT, IMPROVE, MAINTAIN. Commit, right now, to improving your life. Make the changes, one at a time. Consistently maintain those changes, every single day.

STOP BEING AFRAID OF BEING AFRAID. The demons of fear and self-doubt are *predictable*, therefore *manageable*. Fear is part of being human, and courage is *not* the absence of fear. Courage is *facing* fear.

PRACTICE SELF-LOVE AND SELF-ACCEPTANCE. They are the keys to replacing self-defeating attitudes and behaviors with self-*supporting* attitudes and behaviors.

BECOME THE VERY BEST FRIEND YOU EVER HAD IN YOUR LIFE, because your very best friend *has* to be you.

STEVE HAMILTON

TESTIMONIAL

Steve Hamilton is the two-time Edgar Award–winning and *New York Times* bestselling author of the Alex McKnight crime series, the Nick Mason series, and *The Lock Artist*. He has written two *New York Times* Notable Books of the Year and has either won or been nominated for virtually every other award in the business, including the Shamus, Barry, Anthony, Dashiell Hammett Prize, American Library Association Alex Award, CWA Gold Dagger, and the Ian Fleming Steel Dagger. Steve is a graduate of the University of Michigan, where he won the prestigious Hopwood Award for Writing.

"The best chair in America."

When I was helping Greg Harden put this book together, I actually had the idea of including a photograph of the guest chair in his office. I know that sounds strange, but think about it. Throughout Greg's thirty-plus years at the school, every student athlete attending the University of Michigan has had the opportunity to meet with him and to sit in that chair.

If you're finishing this book right now, you know that Tom Brady, the greatest quarterback ever to play the game, sat in that chair. Desmond Howard, who would go on to win the Heisman Trophy and play eleven seasons in the NFL. Charles Woodson, who would also win a Heisman and play eighteen seasons in the NFL, on his way to a Hall of Fame ceremony as probably the best defensive back in NFL history. And at least 350 other players who would go on to the NFL after leaving Michigan, fifty of them drafted in the first round.

At least fifty basketball players who would go on to the NBA, including Tim Hardaway, Jr. and Naismith Award winner Trey Burke. Eighty hockey players who would all have careers in the NHL, including Hobey Baker Award winners Brendan Morrison and Kevin Porter. Twenty baseball players who would make it to the major leagues. And over 120 athletes in other sports who would represent the USA and over twenty other countries in the Olympics—including twenty-three-time gold medalist Michael Phelps, the most decorated Olympian in history.

They all had the chance to sit in that chair.

But just as important are the countless other student athletes who also sat in that chair. Thousands of them, with names you might not know, because they went on to become teachers, counselors, lawyers, doctors, businesspeople. These are the lives that form the true measure of Greg Harden's work and represent the impact he has had on everyone who has ever spent time with him and listened to his message.

It's been one of the great honors of my life to sit in that chair myself, talking to Greg Harden for hours on end, surrounded by the photographs and mementos from his long career. He is a fantastic *listener,* first of all, in a time when listening has become a lost art. When you're sitting in that chair, he focuses on you and nothing else. The door is closed and time slips away, along with everything else in the world waiting outside.

Greg has already changed my life in more ways than I can count, especially with his lessons about recognizing and reprogramming negative self-talk, practicing self-love and self-acceptance, and replacing self-defeating attitudes and behaviors with self-*supporting* attitudes and behaviors.

And more than anything, learning to CONTROL THE CONTROLLABLES— an idea that has never been more important. Focusing on the things right in front of me that I can change, letting go of the things over which I have no control and never will. I can't tell you how much this one lesson has helped me to keep my head on straight while the rest of the world has been turned upside down.

I'll keep coming back to this book for the rest of my life, and I know I'll find something new and valuable every time I read it.

I hope you will, too.

(And thanks, Greg, for letting me sit in that chair!)

CHAPTER 37

THE CHALLENGE:
I Need More from You!

Whenever I counsel people, I know that—at least in the beginning—I will make a point of consistently saying the same things until they start to hear my voice in their heads. Which is fine, but I know that at some point it has to turn into something else. It has to become their own voices inside their own heads, saying the same things in their own way, in their own unique language.

Because ultimately, nothing I've said in this book belongs to me. These are all universal truths. I've just tried to be the vehicle to help you see them in a new way.

More than anything else, I want you to always believe in yourself. But even that is not enough. Right now I want more from you.

This country, this culture, this *world*, is desperately in need of a new kind of leadership. It needs people who want to build each other up, not tear each other down.

Who want to bring people together instead of dividing them even more.

Who want to *invest* in one another, *believe* in one another, and help one another *dream big*, *believe big*, and *become big* in the most positive sense of the word.

As I talked about in "Chapter 3: Control the Controllables!" we need this new way of thinking—this fundamental paradigm shift—now more than ever, as we find ourselves as a society facing not one but two great pandemics. We are challenged *right now* to fight these two formidable enemies at once. It is one of those rare moments that will truly shape our human destiny, and I'm not being hyperbolic when I say that. The stakes really are that high. The history books will record how we respond. I need you to believe that, and I need you to join me in answering this challenge.

I know you're exactly the kind of person who can help make positive things happen. *I know it.* If you have never been needed before, you are sorely needed now. So I'm asking you to help me push the agenda. I'm asking you not to be silent, not to just sit back and process and analyze the world around you. I'm asking you to help *change* the world for the better. Beginning *right now.*

It's a big dream, I know. But if you share in it, you soon realize that the dream itself will never be enough. I need you to believe, not just in yourself, but in the dream, and to make sure that your behavior matches your beliefs, every single day.

Help me spread the word.

Preach it.

Teach it.

Live it.

Every day.

Thank you for giving me the privilege and the honor of sharing these life lessons with you.

Greg Harden

DEDICATION AND ACKNOWLEDGMENTS

This book is dedicated to Howard Brabson, who saw past my many flaws and inconsistencies and dared me to be the man I said I wanted to be. He mentored, pushed, and pulled me to a level of self-awareness and social consciousness that set everything in motion.

To my wife, Shelia M. Harden, who decided I needed someone to check on me and care about me as much as I cared about everyone else. She has influenced and inspired me to take new risks and to give even more than I thought I had to give.

Finally, I dedicate this work with unlimited and unconditional love and appreciation to my parents, Cyrus E. Harden and Kathryn M. Harden. They are now and ever, even when I did not know it, angels. And to all the surrogate parents, mentors, and guardians who guided and protected me throughout my grand adventures, I am grateful beyond my ability to articulate my love, respect, and admiration.

To all of you who were interviewed and contributed in any way to telling the important stories in this book, thank you.

I also want to thank the brilliantly talented Steve Hamilton, who shaped this writer's understanding of what an author looks like and thinks like, and what one must endure. He coached me, trained me, and maneuvered me into taking on this challenge. He is my role model and hero, and a true friend and partner.

Finally, my thanks to Shane Salerno, the hardest-working man in showbiz and beyond. His belief and confidence in my work has been unwavering. He was the one who convinced me that I must create a series of books to capture the essence of my work. His leadership and tenacity are inspirational, and I will always cherish his commitment to staying the course, to destroying all obstacles in my way, and to daring me to reinvent myself.

ABOUT THE AUTHORS

For over thirty years, **GREG HARDEN** built champions as Executive Director of Athletic Counseling at the University of Michigan. Already one of the most influential and well-respected figures in all of college athletics, he saw his national recognition level explode in 2014, when legendary sportscaster James Brown profiled him for the CBS news show *60 Minutes*, calling him "Michigan's Secret Weapon."

Harden has worked with such high-profile athletes as Tom Brady—who he helped go from struggling backup QB to sixth-round NFL draft pick, to seven-time Super Bowl Champion—Heisman Trophy winner and ESPN *College GameDay* cohost Desmond Howard, and Heisman Trophy winner and NFL Hall-of-Famer Charles Woodson. He has counseled over four hundred other student athletes who would go on to professional careers in the four major sports. They include fifty NFL first-round draft picks and 120 Olympic athletes, among them twenty-three-time gold medalist Michael Phelps, the most decorated Olympian in history. But it is the lives of thousands of other people—successful doctors, lawyers, teachers, counselors, broadcasters, businesspeople—that represent the true measure of Greg Harden's work. He continues to offer a powerful message of hope and encouragement in a world that needs it now more than ever.

STEVE HAMILTON is the two-time Edgar Award–winning, *New York Times* bestselling author of the Alex McKnight crime series, the Nick Mason series, and *The Lock Artist*. Steve is a graduate of the University of Michigan, where he won the prestigious Hopwood Award for Writing.